Multiple Perspectives:
A Guide to Qualitative Research
in Music Therapy

Multiple Perspectives:
A Guide to Qualitative Research
in Music Therapy

Henk Smeijsters, Ph.D.

Barcelona PUBLISHERS

This original book is published and distributed by Barcelona Publishers, 4 Whitebrook Road, Lower Village, Gilsum, NH 03448.

ISBN 0-9624080-7-7

First Barcelona Publishers printing November 1997

10 9 8 7 6 5 4 3 2 1

Cover design by Frank McShane
Copyeditor: Katharine O'Moore-Klopf

Printed in the U.S.A.

TABLE OF CONTENTS

Part II: Examples of Qualitative Research in Music Therapy

PREFACE

This book is the result of my exploration of qualitative research methods in music therapy. As a researcher, I based my own qualitative research method on the traditions in The Netherlands. Eventually, I came across qualitative research methods abroad that influenced my own research method and my thoughts about doing research. I decided to write a book to give myself an overview of qualitative possibilities. As one of my professors once said, "If you are searching for knowledge, then write a book about it." It is during the process of writing a book, lecturing about its drafts, and discussing it with colleagues that your own ideas are shaped.

This book is also a continuing dialogue between me and the researchers who presented their work during the first International Symposium for Qualitative Research in Music Therapy (Düsseldorf, 1994). Some of them met again in Berlin in 1996 and during the eighth World Congress of Music Therapy in Hamburg (1996). These colleagues, Ken Aigen, David Aldridge, Dorit Amir, Ken Bruscia, Jörg Frommer, Carolyn Kenny, Mechtild Langenberg, and Even Ruud, inspired me immensely, both personally and professionally. When I was writing this book, I remembered our being together as a group, which Ken Bruscia has described in "Daedalus and the Labyrinth: A Mythical Research Fantasy." He typified me as the group member who takes a compass and a map book to make the mysteries of the labyrinth accessible to us all. Indeed, I want to give you a map of the landscape of qualitative research, but keep in mind that there is not "a" method of qualitative research that I will give you. As in qualitative research itself, there are "multiple perspectives" of research methodology.

Taking part in a dialogue does not mean looking for what is "true" or "false" but assessing the coordinates of your own position in a luxurious landscape of possibilities. When I comment on the research methods developed by colleagues, do not forget that these comments reflect my personal coordinates. I deeply respect my colleagues' work. I comment on their work because I know that together we established a forum where free discussion is possible, where we can debate authentically without promoting our own perspective or being narcissistically wounded by others. Doing research is exciting, and describing and reflecting on the qualitative methods developed in music therapy research is thrilling as well.

In Part I, I start with a summary of the benefits and limitations of quantitative research. In my opinion, music therapy needs both quantitative and qualitative research, but the choice of paradigm depends on the research questions we want to answer. I highlight characteristics of qualitative research and discuss the question of research criteria.

In Part II, each chapter gives an example of a qualitative research method used in music therapy research. First, I point out some general basic characteristics of the method, then illustrate it with an example from specific research. The idea is to look more deeply into the research method and give music therapy researchers a very practical guide how to use it. I also comment on each method from my own perspective.

I hope that music therapy researchers and students can use the book to see what is possible in qualitative research, choose a research method that fits their needs, and plan their research according to the research steps and principles that I describe. My criteria for selection were that the research method was developed and is used by experienced researchers in music therapy, that there has been an article on it published in at least one outstanding international journal, and that the researcher who developed has taken part in actual discussions about qualitative research in music therapy. There are research methods from the United States, the United Kingdom, Germany, and The Netherlands represented here, but this means not that there are no other qualitative research methods but that the research methods included here are those I think are the most current.

Henk Smeijsters, Ph.D.
August 1997

Part I

QUALITATIVE RESEARCH IN GENERAL

Chapter 1

BENEFITS AND LIMITATIONS OF QUANTITATIVE RESEARCH

INTRODUCTION

Most recent research in music therapy is qualitative. In the United States, behaviorism and quantitative research predominated in many specialties for years, but in music therapy, qualitative research became popular because several music therapists became convinced that quantitative research techniques cannot adequately describe music therapy. In Europe, the opposite is true: qualitative research became prominent several decades ago for most specialties, but it has been usurped by quantitative research. Still, new qualitative research methods have emerged in music therapy.

During the First Symposium for Qualitative Research in Düsseldorf, Germany, in summer 1994, participants frequently asked whether quantitative research can describe the essence of music therapy. I believe, however, that music therapy needs both quantitative and qualitative research because each paradigm can answer distinct questions.

This chapter examines the differences between the two methods and presents both their positive and negative sides. Some researchers argue that music therapy needs quantitative methods because they are the only ones that will be accepted by health-insurance providers. This chapter does not consider this argument.

QUANTITATIVE RESEARCH

Characteristics and Benefits

Quantitative research seeks to describe experience in terms of numerals. Numerals tell us something about the existence, nonexistence, frequency, or strength of a phenomenon. They also make it possible to calculate means that summarize the experiences of a number of people.

The people who serve as research subjects form a sample from a population, not from a specific natural context, making the study group artificial instead of naturalistic. In reality, people belong to not one but several different contexts. The benefit of such sampling is that this group is representative of the population, thus allowing us to apply the statistics of the representative sample to the whole population. When we compare two or more groups, the results of tests for statistical significance between the samples hold for the populations.

Quantifying allows us to generalize from a small sample to a large population. With the help of sampling, we can develop a theory about the population. Quantification is the tool we use to develop this universal theory.

Fundamental to this paradigm is the idea that the experiences of people from different places can be described by general concepts and their relationships. This idea holds that people are not unique and that experiences are not context bound, but that there are general laws that can be applied to several people and several contexts.

Before we begin doing quantitative research on a particular point, we already have some sort of general theory consisting of concepts and their relationships. We deduce from this theory several variables that we put into hypotheses formulated to express general laws. With the help of these variables and hypotheses, we study new samples to see if our hypotheses hold true with new material. To test hypotheses, we need a representative sample and an experimental situation in which we can control the variables.

We can summarize the benefits of quantitative research as follows: with the help of quantitative research, we can numerically describe, predict, and test, in a controlled experiment, behavioral processes that we can reduce to variables, that have some general meaning, and that we can thus replicate.

When therapy is the focus of research, quantitative researchers often concentrate on the effects of treatment. It is suggested that "independent" variables lead to effects in "dependent" variables afterward. To ensure that the independent variables cause the effect, researchers establish a control group. This control group resembles the experimental group, differing only in that the independent variables are not included.

We can summarize the benefit of quantitative research for therapy as follows: quantitative research does not describe the whole spectrum of (subjective) effects, but it succeeds in showing with certainty that there is an effect and that the effect is a result of therapy.

Another important characteristic of quantitative research is the method of observation used: we use measuring instruments by which we can quantify observations. We test these instruments for reliability and validity, which means that when the same data are scored at different moments or by different people, the scores will be the same. We ensure reliability and validity also by calculating whether the concepts to be measured correlate with other measures of the same concepts. Because we make no subjective observations or interpretations, we say that we are "objective." When we use measuring instruments during observation, we do not need to use our own subjective resources because we are guided by the measuring instrument. We are not subjectively biased, because our own personal selections and interpretations are excluded. Because the scales are standardized, every measurement looks the same. The same questions are answered and the same behaviors are scored each time. This sameness makes it possible for us to compare behaviors occurring at different times or in different persons. To see if a client changes over time, we compare the same behaviors over time; to see if several clients share the same problems, we compare the same behaviors.

The benefit of quantitative research is that objective registrations and comparisons become possible. For examples of quantitative research in music therapy, see Standley and Prickett (1994), Hanser and Wheeler (1995), Hanser (1995), and Lathom-Radocy and Radocy (1995).

Limitations

We now turn to some of the limitations of quantitative research. When a client is depressed, there is a preexisting preverbal psychological and physiological state of mind. When the client tries to find a word for this state, this is the first step of abstraction: the word is not precisely the same as the state of mind. When we ask the client to use a numeral to rate his or her state of mind, this is a further abstraction. Although this numeral reduces the experience to a mere value, it makes it possible for us to describe a general aspect shared by different people. When *depression* becomes a numeral between 1 and 10 on a scale, then it becomes possible to quantify how many people score a particular number, the mean score for a group of people, and so on.

This benefit also includes a limitation: quantitative research simplifies experience. What does a numeral say about the real experience of depression? Of course, tests developed to measure depression are not based on a single numeral. A lot of items can be scored. Nevertheless, such a standardized way of observing can never fully describe the experience of a particular client. A lot of words are needed to approach the preverbal experience of depression. It has often been argued that the Romanticists described depression better and let us feel what it really is better than do psychological tests. This same argument has been used by music therapists, understandably so because music therapists know that musical sounds can very nearly express the preverbal experiences of the client.

We might conclude that an individual client needs a flexible measuring instrument that is as close as possible to the personal experience. Qualitative researchers conclude that the human being is the most flexible measuring instrument.

When discussing quantitative methods, we must question not only reductionism but also the use of group means. What does a group mean tell us about personal processes? In a way, a group mean is not real but an artificial score that does not exist as an individual score. For instance, when one client's score changes from 5 to 8 and another's changes from 5 to 2, then the mean of 8 and 2 is 5, making it seem as if there were no change.

Another concern about quantitative research centers around measuring effects only. Of course we need to study effects —without effects, any discussion about music therapy is meaningless—but what is really important are the processes that lead to the effects. Human beings are not black boxes, with music therapy as input and its behavioral effects as output. Human beings are very complex, continually developing creatures in whom many processes influence and interact with one another. Effects are only the final points of the developing process, and a real understanding of music therapy requires insight into this process and the way music therapy is linked to the aspects of the process.

What is more, not only is using a numeral to describe an experience an abstraction, using samples is an abstraction as well. Samples do not "exist"; they are artificial combinations of people from a conceptualized population. In reality, we find groups of people who are related to one another who share the same context.

Quantitative research is atomistic; that is, it assumes the individuals selected from a population and put into a group represent a natural human group that is characterized by the melting together of people into a social gestalt. Of course, when research is not conducted in order to observe group patterns, this might not be a problem, but when—as in music therapy—the music group is an essential means of therapy, then a "representative" sample is not representative because it does not reflect a natural group.

Another point should be mentioned: representativity is possible only through reductionism. For example, a group of depressed patients can be labeled as such only because every person is reduced to a depressed person. We can divide the human race into women and men and by doing so make every woman be representative of all women. Mutatis mutandis, a depressed client can represent a group of depressives. One woman, however, is not precisely like another, and one depressed person is not like another. I am not claiming that there is an extreme uniqueness, only arguing that representativity is limited.

The claim for objectivity in quantitative research means observing without empathy and interpretation. Is it possible, though, to understand human beings without being empathic, without making inferences about internal states and meaning of behaviors? In psychotherapy, these aspects count, so if they are left out of research, what can research give us? Let me go a little bit further. If it is true that objectivity is impossible because observation changes what is being observed, then is an experiment in which the therapy situation is manipulated to isolate independent variables really studying what it was aimed to? No; instead, it researches a manipulated research object.

In-depth discussions about differences between quantitative and qualitative research in music therapy have been put forward by Aigen (1993), Bruscia (1995a), and Smeijsters (1996b, 1996c, 1996d, 1996e).

QUANTITATIVE SINGLE-CASE RESEARCH

Sometimes implementing an experimental design—intended to control for internal validity—is impossible because several difficulties, such as the following, arise:

- It is impossible to establish experimental and control groups by randomization or matching because clients normally go into therapy within their own living group. The between-group differences might thus be strong.
- It is impossible to arrange homogeneous groups. The within-group differences are thus strong.
- It is impossible to control treatment. Independent variables change because of the treatment process. If control is possible, treatment is no longer naturalistic.
- It is impossible to assess treatment variables that are too complex.
- It is impossible to solve the ethical problem of giving no treatment to the control group.
- It is impossible to develop an adequate placebo as a control.
- It is impossible to control by measuring instruments for all personal variables that might be important.

A solution to some problems posed by the quantitative experimental group design is to use a single-case design. A growing interest in this type of research has been shown in recent literature (Aldridge, 1994, 1996; Cook and Campbell, 1979; Hilliard, 1993; Kiesler, 1983; Strupp, 1990;).

Hilliard (1993) defines *single-case research* as intrasubject research, which focuses on changes over time within a single person. Generalization is possible not by means of representative samples but by means of replication of single-case findings. Single-case research can be observational or experimental. Data gathering can be quantitative or qualitative. Qualitative single-case research is discussed in the following chapters.

Isolating variables can be problematic with this type of research, too, because a therapeutic process cannot be reduced to changing just single variables. When research should represent "real therapy," then the therapy should be able to change every moment when the client and/or therapist feels this is needed. Also often missing from a treatment theory are a definition of the variables from which deductions can be made and reliable scales by which to measure these variables.

If we use an experimental single-case design despite these drawbacks, then at least it should be clear:

- That we have outlined the essential ingredients of the music therapy method chosen
- That we have applied this method adequately
- That we can apply baseline measures
- That we will use the music therapy method at different times, with different people, in different situations

The rationale of the experimental single-case study is that when an effect occurs at different times, in different situations, and with different people, it is unlikely that it is caused by something from outside that runs synchronously with the repeated introduction of treatment. It is likely that the effect has been caused by the music therapy method that each time has been introduced just before the effect. By repeatedly taking baseline measurements and introducing the treatment, we can control internal validity. The "experimental group" is the total of scores of one individual during treatment periods; the "control group" is the total of scores of baseline periods.

Two possible designs are the reversal and the multiple baseline. For examples from music therapy, see Wheeler, 1995. In both designs, there is a baseline from which we can assess the behavior of the client before treatment. Through comparison with a mean baseline score, we can conclude that an extreme score at the beginning biases the effect measure at the end. For instance, if the pretreatment score incidentally was extremely low or extremely high, this score at the end will be more moderate, independent of treatment.

In the reversal design, the treatment is introduced after a baseline score is obtained. After the first treatment period, a baseline score without treatment is reestablished After this baseline period, treatment is reintroduced. If there is an effect only during treatment, we can conclude that the treatment causes the effect; however, interpretation is difficult when the effect does not decrease during repeated baseline testing. Then it is possible that maturation or an external cause that coincided with the first introduction of treatment is responsible for the effect. If, however, the effect decreases during repeated baseline periods, this signifies that other problems have arisen. How important is an effect of music therapy when it immediately diminishes after treatment has been withdrawn? Is it ethically justified to introduce a baseline when treatment shows an effect?

Another problem with these measures is that the human being is supposed to be some sort of a stimulus–response machine. Examples of the reversal design from music therapy show that the behaviors that are monitored (for instance, eye contact, on-task behavior, cooperation) are very simple. If deeper psychological processes are involved, it is difficult to suggest that these processes react as is supposed in the reversal design.

The multiple baseline is not obstructed by the ethical problems of the reversal design. Treatment is introduced at different times with different clients. Again, it is unlikely that a factor from outside exactly coincides with the introduction of treatment at different times. The "experimental group" is the total number of scores from different clients when treatment has been introduced. The "control group" is composed of the total of baseline scores from different clients.

When working with one client, we can use a treatment in different situations or for different behaviors. Again, this shows that a person is seen as an associanistic cumulation of independent behaviors. For instance, we can introduce the treatment first to increase task behavior and then later to decrease disturbing behavior. Alternatively, with social behavior we first work to focus social behavior during classroom time, and then after some time, during spare time.

The examples in current literature (Kazdin, 1986; Hanser, 1987; and Hanser, 1995) are convincing. Psychological processes cannot be split up into distinct aspects of behavior or distinct situational behavior, however. We choose a treatment for depression to influence the depression as a whole, not as a cumulation of depressive symptoms. Most of the examples belong to situations in which behavior easily can be quantified. The quantifiability of distinct behavioral aspects leads to quantitative reversal and multiple baseline designs. We can conclude that if both characteristics are there, these design can be used very well and can solve the problems of the quantitative experimental group design. If the therapy situation is different, then we should not use these designs; perhaps we must consider a qualitative research method.

Group designs and experimental single-case designs both belong to the quantitative paradigm because the researcher tries to see if independent variables cause changes in dependent variables. Thus, the impossibility of experimental group designs points to qualitative research, although not immediately. We must consider the possibility of experimental single-case designs. If these are impossible, because, for instance, it makes no sense to isolate variables and qualitative research is needed, then we have to consider that using the qualitative paradigm is not just another way to look for causal relationships.

Qualitative thinking is different because there are no abstractions, there is no reductionism, there are no isolated variables, no causal relationships, no effects, and so on. I am not saying that abstractions, fragmentations, or reductions are "bad." What I mean is that it depends on what you want to know and what fits the therapy situation best.

CONCLUSION

The quantitative paradigm makes it possible to research whether something (a mean score of an excerpt of behavior) changes, whether this change is caused by something, whether this change is a result of misinterpretation, and whether this change can replicated under the same circumstances. Whether a reality that is reduced by measuring instruments and preestablished theory resembles a naturalistic situation, what the meaning is of measurement scores, how the process of change took place, whether the experimental manipulation resembles a naturalistic therapy process, how an individual changes, and whether changes in one person resemble changes in another person are questions that cannot be answered easily by using quantitative research methods.

Chapter 2

CHARACTERISTICS OF
QUALITATIVE RESEARCH*

DIFFERENCES BETWEEN THE QUANTITATIVE
AND QUALITATIVE PARADIGMS

Quantitative Methodology

This chapter focuses mainly on quantitative experiments. In quantitative research, we deduce a hypothesis from a theory. The hypothesis describes the relationship between two theoretical concepts called variables. Independent variables may affect dependent variables.

To test the relationship between variables, we must operationalize them. We operationalize an independent variable, which is supposed to affect a dependent variable, by precisely describing a procedure that has to be followed as described and cannot be changed during research. We operationalize the dependent variable by using a measuring instrument that is standardized, objective, reliable, and validated and can be quantified:

- *Standardization* means that we use the structure and items the same way each time.
- *Objective* means that we do not include our subjective impressions or interpretations that we cannot describe in concrete behavior.

---

*Portions of this chapter are modified from Smeijsters (1996e), with permission.

- *Reliable* means that two independent observers obtain the same score or that repetition of scoring—contextual things being equal—leads to same scores.
- *Valid* means that the score correctly quantifies what it was meant to measure.

We then use scores collected with these measuring instruments to calculate whether differences are statistically significant, which means that we can generalize them to the population from which we took the sample. When calculating, we combine scores of individuals in mean scores.

Because we study only the effect of the independent variables, we design an experiment in which in we introduce the independent variables in the experimental group and omit them in the control group, all other possible independent variables being equal in both groups.

Reliability, validity, and other concepts have a different meaning in qualitative research than in quantitative research. This is discussed in the next chapter.

Qualitative Methodology

Of course, the description of quantitative research I gave in Chapter 1 is very limited. For more information, read books on quantitative methodology.

In qualitative research, no theory leads the research process. On the contrary, theories are developed from the therapy. Qualitative researchers argue that there can be no "general theory"—only "practical" theories that take care of the context-bound individual and multilevel features of practice. They do not believe that general laws are central to all specific practical events; they believe instead that these general laws can be found in an experimental laboratory situation that acts as a artificial representation of the real world.

Contexts can be described as being specific and not representative or complex and not reducible to variables. Qualitative researchers suggest neither that there can be clear, defined independent and dependent variables that can be studied nor that treatment can be manipulated so that only selected independent variables will change. They believe that in space and time, there are no points alike. For them, there is no possible replication in space and time; thus, there can be no sampling and no generalization. *Sampling* means that the part is representative for the whole, and *generalization* means that the whole is reflected in the part. In qualitative thinking, there is not "the" reality, "the" whole, "the" part, but multiple realities, many different wholes and different parts. In quantitative research, however, there is a search for "truth." Because of this, experiences that do not lead to truth—in which it is not possible that one event can falsify the other—are excluded from quantitative research.

Quantitative researchers focus on "something" that has been abstracted, but qualitative researchers focus on the unabstracted whole. If we see our thinking process as a line, then at one end there is the unique, described as a whole and therefore different from each other object, and at the other end there is the abstraction, a reduction of all unique wholes and therefore representative of them.

If we focus on the whole of one particular context, then it would not be logical to use a general theory and deduce hypotheses from it. This explains why qualitative researchers develop hypotheses from context (see Chapter 5, Grounded Theory). For this, they need an "open" research attitude (see Chapter 4, under the section General Principles of Phenomenology). Concepts and hypotheses are not preestablished, and as Lincoln and Guba point out, sometimes qualitative researchers do not even know what they want to know or what they do not know (Lincoln and Guba, 1995). The qualitative research attitude is inductive: hypotheses are generated and not "tested."

Instead of taking a representative sample of a population, qualitative researchers take an example from practice. By giving a detailed description, they can use this example to gain insight into whether another case is alike and where differences can be found. They focus on naturalistic intrasubjective processes rather than on effects obtained by artificial means.

For the quantitative researcher, there is no personal view. Things are as they are—objective, and everyone, by replicated observation, can verify the researcher's findings. It is easy to see why, then, that behaviorism, which aims to focus on objective behavior, was adopted eagerly by quantitative researchers. If the researcher wants to understand the meaning of these behaviors and must interpret them, however, quantitative research falls short. Music therapy researchers who believe behavior is not the "essence" of music therapy therefore reject quantitative research. Often, they do not believe that thoughts, feelings, and intuitions can be studied using standardized (objective) assessment scales. The critics of quantitative research seem to identify quantitative research with behaviorism. In the next chapter, we will also see that fundamental research criteria often seem to be identified with quantitative research techniques.

Qualitative researchers use the person as a subjective tool to research experience. The person, not the assessment scale, is the instrument because multiple aspects, complexity, and changes can best be registered by a human being. Researchers argue that there should not be a subject-object dichotomy, that instead, the researcher interacts as a person with another person, thus verifying that naturalistic theory is indeed grounded in personal experience. They reject such a dichotomy, postulated by physicists before the advent of quantum physics, because quantum physics teaches that knowledge depends on context.

Because music therapists are most close to the therapeutic context in qualitative research, the roles of music therapist, observer, and researcher are often filled by one person. If the person who is most committed to the client is most able to "research," then is it impossible for a nonparticipating person to understand what is going on? If you need countertransferential feelings to understand the client's feelings, are you able to feel these when you are not in the situation yourself?

In qualitative research, there are no assessment scales, no figures, but there is a precise description that is analyzed for content, coded, and categorized. We ensure "validity" and "reliability" by using such techniques as triangulation, member checking, peer debriefing, pattern matching, controlled subjectivity, repeated observation, and replication of the chain of evidence (Lincoln and Guba, 1985).

We can summarize by saying that qualitative researchers' concept of reality and how this reality can be researched differs from that of quantitative researchers. There is no artificial situation in which isolated variables of reality are studied within a model of reality. In qualitative research, we do not manipulate phenomena by experimental procedures to control variables.

Qualitative research is about organic, dynamic, multiple, complex, and idiosyncratic realities. To understand these multiple realities, we must understand and interact subjectively and use a research design that is not predetermined but can be accommodated to natural reality. The research design and techniques are processes, as is the treatment itself. As a result, there is no gap between research findings and clinical significance.

Qualitative research is descriptive, which means that we describe a phenomenon as fully as possible with words. There is no measuring instrument that operationally reduces a phenomenon so that it reflects only a part of itself. The intrasubjective experiences of study participants, instead of objectification, are the research focus. At the beginning of a qualitative research project, we use no existing theoretical concepts, because it is difficult to subsume specific aspects of practice under theoretical concepts developed to allow generalizations across situations. Open coding ensures that our theorizing fits the natural process as well as possible. Qualitative research is inductive and generates hypotheses, thus making theory out of practice. We view the phenomenon not as a sample from a population to which we can generalize our findings but as an example to which we can compare other examples.

QUALITATIVE RESEARCH TECHNIQUES

Chapter 3 discusses in more depth the question of "reliability" and "validity" in qualitative research. Here, I give only general descriptions of techniques used in qualitative research.

Subjectivity

Qualitative researchers believe that excluding subjective experiences (feelings, thoughts, images, intuitions) produces only a very limited description of participants' personal processes. Subjectivity must be included; therefore, personal experience becomes an important focus of qualitative research.

When we incorporate subjectivity instead of objectivity, the question is then whether and how we can check for subjectivity. In qualitative methodology, we can use several methods.

CONTROLLED SUBJECTIVITY. With so-called controlled subjectivity, researchers are trained—by supervision—to explore their own countertransference (Tüpker, 1990b).

REPEATED OBSERVATION BY THE SAME RESEARCHER. Another possibility involves repeated observations made by the same researcher—for instance, when the music therapist and the researcher are the same person. During music therapy, the music therapist may experience thoughts, feelings, images, and so on. He or she records the session and reviews the recording after some time, noting feelings during the review. If he or she feels differently, this does not mean that either the feelings that occurred during the initial therapy session or those generated by the review are "wrong." It is just that there are different emotional perspectives.

REPEATED ANALYSIS. *Repeated analysis* involves researchers' regularly comparing old data with new, thus checking their previous hypotheses. They can also check whether the old data corroborate their latest interpretations, whether previous interpretations need to be changed, or whether previous interpretations can be used for old data, but new data require new interpretations.

OPEN-MINDEDNESS. Some qualitative researchers make use of open-mindedness (receptivity), described by Smaling (1995) as "... the ability or capacity of the mind for receiving impressions ... to undo (your) listening and also experiencing in general from some culturally learned habits." When we use open-mindedness, our concepts are adjusted to fit nature and not the other way around. Finding the concepts that fit a particular situation is one of the aims of qualitative research.

CATEGORIZATION. It is advisable to make complete transcripts of all observations, interviews, recordings, and so forth. Over time, some words in the transcript may seem important to you, so mark these words. They can become sensitizing concepts (Glaser and Strauss, 1967) that guide the selection of words in forthcoming transcripts. These concepts always are tentative. After they have been established, they give direction to the process of data selection, but you will adjust them when, because you are being open-minded, data point in another direction.

Sensitizing concepts can give rise to the development of categories, which are "boxes" resulting from the comparison of pieces of data with each other. You group together in the same box those words that appear to refer to a similar phenomenon (Strauss and Corbin, 1990). For instance, you can place sentences referring to diagnosis into a diagnostic category. Comments on aims can form a category, as can notes about interaction, emotions, thoughts, images, and so on. Categories can be subdivided into subcategories. In grounded theory, the research process generates categories. Some qualitative researchers, however, make use of preestablished categories.

ANALYTICAL MEMOS. After each session, researchers can write several analytical memos (Ely et al., 1995), using categories and marked words that can become part of a category. In these memos, researchers hypothesize about which category the marked words belong to, developing a diagnostic theme, for instance. Ely et al. (1995) define a theme as a ". . . statement of meaning that runs through all or most of the pertinent data."

Other marked words can give rise to questions about music therapists' objectives, play forms, and techniques; the link between diagnosis and treatment; and therapists' therapeutic attitudes. Researchers can also use analytical memos to make inferences about clients' personal experiences during musical activity and to propose alternative suggestions to music therapists as to how to proceed with treatment.

Analytical memos are a means of stimulating music therapists' reflections during treatment. On the other hand, music therapists and/or observers comment on them, so they aid in checking the researchers' data processing and interpretations. Because this process of feedback between music therapist, researcher, and observer is circular and is repeated many times, it is called circular iterative feedback.

MEMBER CHECKING. This feedback is part of member checking: checking the data, themes, interpretations, and conclusions with the very people we are studying, especially music therapists and clients (Lincoln and Guba, 1985; Ely et al, 1995). When, for example, a therapist thinks that improvisations open up feelings for the client, it is important to know whether the client experiences it that way. Of course, there is one problem here: if the expression of feelings happens unconsciously and the client is not aware of these expressed feelings, then he or she might react by saying, "I didn't feel anything," even though the music therapist may be convinced that the client did express feelings. Because of this, I advocate having at least one person besides the music therapist and the client participate in member checking. If this person—the researcher—also independently feels that the improvisation in question sounded different and if the client did not express these feelings in previous sessions, then perhaps it is reasonable to suggest that improvising made expression possible (see, for instance, Smeijsters and van den Hurk, in press).

In one single-case study, the client—a woman with musicogenic epilepsy (Smeijsters and van den Berk, 1995)—several times corrected the interpretations of the music therapist and the researcher. For instance, she questioned the hypotheses that movement could guard against epileptic fits, that her fits were evoked by associations, and that she would be able to influence the fit at the beginning.

Member checking with the therapy client not only assesses the credibility of the research findings, it also becomes part of treatment. The music therapist must therefore decide whether and at what time member checking can contribute to the therapeutic process and must introduce and discuss it with the client during the session.

Whereas the transcripts of tapes, discussions, and interviews contain only manifest data, analytical memos make interpretations and draw conclusions on a deeper level. They are tentative, will often be changed, and can be of less importance when therapy proceeds. It is advisable, then, to exclude analytical memos from member checking with the client during therapy.

Peer Debriefing

Peer debriefing (Lincoln and Guba, 1985) or *peer checking* (Ely et al., 1995) means questioning biases and testing working hypotheses by asking independent experts to check the descriptions and give meaning to the data. These experts are not involved with the treatment or the research; they only receive the complete research report and are asked to challenge the data analysis. For instance, when I was researching musicogenic epilepsy (Smeijsters and van den Berk, 1995), I contacted several neurologists so I could learn more about epilepsy and musicogenic epilepsy. With this information, I was able to make hypotheses about how music therapy could be of benefit.

The use of different personal sources (the client, the music therapist, the researcher, the observer, the expert), the use of different data-collecting techniques (self-reports, observation reports, discussions, interviews), and the exploration of several theoretical models are part of triangulation (Lincoln and Guba, 1985).

Pattern Matching

Pattern matching or *structural corroboration* (Guba and Lincoln, 1985; Yin, 1989) refers to the procedure of predicting that specific phenomena—treatment aspects, experiential and behavioral aspects—form an integrated pattern. This procedure closely corresponds to the formulation of outcome goals, which is done in clinical practice and is similar to the process of prediction used in quantitative research.

In clinical practice, music therapists predict what changes they expect in clients' musical playing, their behaviors, and their experiences if treatment is "effective." Music therapists choose play forms and techniques through which they believe they can contribute to these effects. For instance, if a music therapist uses an expressive technique such as asking the client to find sounds that fit his or her moods, then the therapist hopes, believes, and predicts that the expressive qualities of the client's sounds will change over time, that the client will speak more openly about feelings, will be able to remember feelings, and will describe the emotional quality of relationships.

If, as a second example, the client is unable to introduce any kind of structure into his or her music playing, the therapist might predict that by improvising on polarities (such as "hot/cold"), the client will eventually spontaneously develop musical form.

Another example can help us understand how music therapy and nonmusical behavior can form a pattern. When I was researching the treatment of a client with compulsive personality disorder (van den Hurk and Smeijsters, 1991; Smeijsters and van den Hurk, 1994), I believed there were strong analogies (Smeijsters, in press) between the client's experimental musical improvisations and his behaviors outside music therapy. It seemed credible that some of his behaviors, such as not being upset when locked up in an elevator, deciding spontaneously to drive his car to the garage, taking vacations without making an endless list of precautions to be taken, and deciding to alter his relationships, were connected to his free musical improvisations in music therapy.

Although this line of reasoning resembles the quantitative paradigm, it is not the same as the independent and dependent variables of quantitative research. A pattern is a complex of phenomena that are put together; it is a "structure" that is "constructed." There is no experiment; there is no search for a linear causal relationship. There *is* the construction of a credible interrelational complexity, corroborated by the participants.

Time-Series Analysis

Similar to pattern matching is time-series analysis, in which we assume that there is a particular sequence of treatment phases. For instance, in the case of the client with the compulsive personality disorder mentioned above, the process of working through grief in music therapy started with the exploration of musical elements, which made possible the client's musical expression of feelings. In a subsequent case (Smeijsters and Van den Berk, 1995), the researchers' hypothesis was affirmed that first concentrating on musical processes contributed to the evocation of hidden feelings.

Multiple-Case Studies and Replication

The multiple-case study (Miles and Huberman, 1984) makes use of parallel cases in which treatment starts at different times. If changes occur only during or after treatment episodes, it is likely that there is a link between changes and treatment processes. "Replication" is literal when the "same" treatment method is repeated in a new case. Theoretical replication is possible when we adjust treatment to clients' needs and predict which other changes will take place (Yin, 1989). Theoretical replication can also take uniqueness into account.

The mandate of "replication" can be fulfilled after the completion of research by having a second researcher replicate the chain of evidence. So that this is possible, researchers must record all data, categories, themes, interpretations, and conclusions in a research report (Yin, 1989). In articles, which are much more limited than research reports, they should use a structure that shows how the data and interpretations developed, so that readers can check the reasoning. A research report should include:

- Transcripts of all self-reports by the music therapist and client, observation reports by the observer(s), transcripts of discussions within the research team, transcripts from evaluative interviews the music therapist had with the client, and transcripts from peer debriefings with the independent experts
- Categories that emerged and guided data analysis developed by the researcher
- The researcher's analytical memos and the music therapist's and observer's feedback to these memos
- Themes generated by the researcher from marked words in the transcripts and categories, validated by other members of the research team
- Generated hypotheses—about indications, goals and objectives, play forms, and techniques of music therapy— established by the members of the research team
- The local diagnostic theory, constructed as a result of content analysis of the whole set of sessions, developed by tho rooonrohor
- Hypotheses about progress, patterns, essences, and so on, formulated by the members of the research team
- Guidelines (rules of thumb that may be used in similar cases) suggested by the researcher and validated by other members of the research team
- Hypotheses about the role of music, generated by the therapist and established by the researcher

CONCLUSION

Choosing a qualitative single-case method does not relieve researchers of the obligation to comply with scientific criteria. There are certain questions fundamental to scientific criteria: Has the phenomenon been represented as completely as possible? Has it been adequately conceptualized? Is enough known about factors influencing the phenomenon? In what respects is the phenomenon similar to or different from other phenomena? In the next chapter, we will discuss these criteria in more detail.

Chapter 3

"RELIABILITY" AND "VALIDITY" IN QUALITATIVE SINGLE-CASE RESEARCH*

This chapter discusses the necessity for doing qualitative single-case research. *Qualitative research* refers to a method aimed at describing and conceptualizing processes within music therapy occurring in a natural therapeutic setting, uninfluenced by research (Bogdan and Biklen, 1982). *Single-case* means that the object of study is an individual client or group.

QUALITATIVE SINGLE-CASE RESEARCH

Recently, psychotherapy researchers have given considerable attention to single-case research (Cook and Campbell, 1979; Hilliard, 1993; Kiesler, 1983; Strupp, 1990). Some psychotherapists have criticized current methods of effect measurement in groups because they are of little value in studying the process of change. This process is an individual event with more phases than are represented in pre- and post-tests. A single test at the end of treatment does not yield sufficient information for the therapist to understand an effect (Greenberg, 1986). Obviously, small changes take place during the process, and it is precisely the study of the process and its changes that offers insight into how change occurs and what triggers it.

---

*Portions of this chapter are modified from Smeijsters (1996e), with permission.

The experimental-group approach in particular has been criticized for other reasons, too, such as the heterogeneity of the clients within and across both the experimental and control groups, ethical and internal validity problems regarding the control group, the complexity of and limited possibilities for manipulating variables in a therapy situation, and the importance of the context within which these variables occur (Greenberg, 1986; Kazdin, 1986). Hutjes and van Buuren (1992) have criticized surveys because these incorporate only a limited number of isolated variables, thus detracting from the complexity of the natural situation. Consequently, experiments and surveys involving groups often lack adequate relevance for therapeutic situations.

Single-case research has come to be conceived as a legitimate alternative. As has been stated in a previous chapter, Hilliard (1993) defines *single-case research* as intrasubject research that focuses on the individual's internal changes over time. Research design can be either experimental or observational, and data processing can be quantitative or qualitative. The approach can be either one that tests hypotheses or one that generates them. As mentioned before, isolating variables and subjecting the client to an experimental procedure is not always feasible or desirable because the main purpose of the therapy is to benefit the client, meaning it must always be open to adaptation. Above all, manipulation of variables implies that the variables are known and that there is a theory from which hypotheses can be drawn to explicitly formulate the relationships between the variables beforehand. Quantification is possible and desirable only if numerical measuring instruments are available that do justice to the observed phenomenon.

The observational, qualitative, hypothesis-generating, single-case approach is adequate for music therapy because experimental designs are difficult to implement in existing practice situations and because the music therapy process has to be able to develop freely (Aigen, 1993).

There are not yet any sufficiently reliable, valid instruments available (Aldridge, 1993), and standardized tests cannot always give a complete picture of the situation. There is also no discernible theory from which to derive variables and hypotheses (Remmert, 1992). The methods of treatment developed can serve as hypotheses to be subjected at a later stage to experimental, hypothesis-testing, and possibly quantitative single-case research.

There are many traditional case studies of music therapy, but the amount of qualitative single-case research, concurrent with the latest developments, has steadily increased in recent years (Aigen, 1995a; Amir, 1990, 1992, 1993, 1996a; Bruscia, 1995b; Forinash, 1990, 1992; Forinash and Gonzalez, 1989; Gonzalez, 1992; Kenny, 1989, 1996; Langenberg et al., 1992, 1993, 1996; Smeijsters et al., 1993, 1994, 1995, 1996a; Tüpker, 1988).

A separate point, made by Bogdan and Biklen (1982), among others, is worthy of special attention because it is often argued explicitly by music therapists and music therapy researchers. It is the view that qualitative research is concerned with "meaning" rather than "truth." It has often been suggested that the essence of music therapy—identified as that which is experienced by the music therapist and the client during music therapy (Forinash and Gonzalez, 1989; Hesser, 1982)—is lost in quantitative research. This assertion raises new questions, however: Does the essence of music therapy consist only of the experiences of the music therapist and the client, or is it just as much the process and the musical events (Bruscia, 1996a)? Does the essence also include demonstrable nonexperiential effects? A strong emphasis on the music therapist's experience seems particularly open to question (Forinash, 1993). This chapter discusses how the subjective experiences of the music therapist and music therapy researcher can be monitored methodologically.

NONSCIENTIFIC CASE STUDIES

One way to study individual cases in natural situations is the traditional case study. This type of study is generally not afforded much scientific status, however, because it does not meet the requirements considered important for research (Kazdin, 1986). For instance, it is unclear how much of what is reported in a case study as being the therapeutic process is in fact the result of conscious or unconscious subjective selection by the therapist. The therapist is the one who decides which data are included in the report; there is no system of checks and balances involving either the therapist or his or her colleagues. We do not know which material would have been presented had the therapist gone through the process a second time or had there been another participating therapist describing what was going on. It is also uncertain whether the therapist encodes the selected data correctly and whether the description and interpretation fit what is being described. This problem is equally relevant to both treatment and progress. There is no check on the process of conceptualization. We do not know which concepts would have been used if the therapist had been able to conceptualize from a different perspective or if another therapist or researcher had participated. As readers of the report, we have only selected encoded data, and the final form of the report makes it seem as if the way the therapist handled the case was the only way to do it. We do not have the original data to see if selections and concepts were grounded in the data. We take for granted and trust the processes of selecting and encoding, but we are not able to verify them. Incomplete representation of data can result in the unjustified suggestion of a link between treatment and progress and increase the likelihood of overlooking alternative explanations. We can believe that it was the particular therapy used that led to results, but when selections and encodings already can be victims of bias, then any connections we make between them can be biased, too. Case studies provide readers with insufficient information to be able to check the accuracy of the conclusions.

Because of all the various possible distortions caused by selection, incorrect descriptions, and arbitrary links, this type of case study has to be labeled nonscientific. I am saying not that therapists who undertake case studies are misleading themselves and others, but that the problem is that we cannot replicate the chain of evidence of their reasoning. We have only selections, concepts, and their interconnections, which, on the surface, seem to fit together—but we cannot look under the surface. In my opinion, research needs procedures that give insight into the relationships between surface and subtext. By using the concepts of "reliability" and "validity," we can take a more detailed look at these above-mentioned problems (Campbell and Stanley, 1966; Hutjes and van Buuren, 1992; Yin, 1989). (When "reliability," "validity," and other concepts in this chapter are in quotation marks, this is because their meaning for qualitative researchers is different from their meaning for quantitative researchers. These differences are discussed later in this chapter.)

Research is "reliable" as long as the selection of material is neither arbitrary nor dependent on coincidence. For example, there is a risk that when we watch a videotape of a music therapy session, we will observe completely different data each time we see the tape. If there is only one observer who carries out a single observation without using any tests, then the resulting data depend on the chance selection that the observer makes at that one moment. The images and sounds the tape has recorded should be registered, as far as is possible, independent of any coincidence. If data are determined by chance, then conclusions based on this information have little scientific significance.

Construct validity refers to the accurate representation of events by the constructs used to describe them. Problems with construct validity are common in music therapy whenever musical processes are described using terminology derived from psychotherapy. Different music therapists can describe the same musical event using completely different theoretical models. This in itself is not necessarily contradictory, because a situation can be viewed from various perspectives; however, if the same detail is given entirely different labels, then the "construct validity" might be dubious.

Internal validity refers to whether processes of change can be linked to therapeutic procedures—that is, has music therapy contributed to the client's improvement? In a traditional research design using an experimental and a control group, the potential influence of such factors as simultaneous events, maturation, spontaneous recovery, statistical regression, and the influence of repeated measurement (Campbell and Stanley, 1966) is accounted for because we can assess it by looking at the control group. Because the case study has no control group, the therapist often merely describes what happens during the therapy and concludes that when progress occurs, it is connected to the treatment that preceded it. Almost no consideration is given to competing variables and alternative explanations.

Because there is no representative sample taken from a population, the "external validity" of a case study—that is, the applicability of the results to other situations—is unknown. On the other hand, because the natural situation is not manipulated, the case study's similarity to other practice situations is greater than to experimental situations.

SCIENTIFIC CASE STUDIES

The qualitative, nonexperimental scientific case study does not rely on statistical tests and treatment of the client under study is not manipulated. How, then, can "reliability" and "validity" be ensured?

"Reliability"

In a number of examples of qualitative music therapy research, the personal impressions of the client and the therapist are considered very important (Aigen, 1993; Amir, 1990; Ferrara, 1984; Forinash, 1993; Forinash and Gonzalez, 1989; Osborne, 1989; Tüpker, 1990b). In the phenomenological tradition, the individual's experience—how the situation "appears" to the person—forms the point of departure. In classic phenomenological research, the principle of phenomenological reduction keeps this experience "open," or unaffected by any *a priori* theoretical model.

As already mentioned, experience is often considered the core of therapy in the experience-oriented school of music therapy research. The essence of music therapy is considered to be the personal experiences—for instance, the images and feelings—of the client and the music therapist. The role of researcher can be filled in several ways. The researcher and the music therapist can be the same person, the researcher can act as a participating observer alongside the music therapist, or the researcher can adopt a role distinct from the subjects. In the former two instances, the researcher's experiences are also included in the data.

When music therapists, as researchers, use their experiences as methodological principles and hold the opinion that "objectivity" obstructs the subjectivity needed to understand the essential music therapy process, they ignore the fact that *subjectivity* has two distinct meanings here. Personal impressions make it possible for us to comprehend the meaning of an improvisation, but *subjective* also means coincidental, or "valid" for only one person. Rejecting "objectivity" should not mislead us into accepting the researcher's subjectivity as the only source. To clarify, I am saying not that we need "objectivity" but that if a researcher uses only his or her own subjectivity, then we need procedures by which we can determine which other perspectives can reflect the phenomenon, whether the researcher's perspective is biased by countertransference, whether it is influenced by incidental moods, and so forth. Doing research for me always means checking. There is not a "truth"; there may be different perspectives from one or several people.

In a strictly phenomenological sense, only the client's experience is important. Reality is perceived as the client perceives it. There is little point in measuring one client's personal reality against another client's personal reality. That kind of "objectivity" would ignore the individual nature of each perception. When a process involving a client is subjected to an experience-oriented process of perception carried out by someone else, however, it is important that this process comprise more than just one observer's personal perception at any one moment in time. Some form of inter- or intrasubjective replication is essential from the point of view of research.

There can be no guarantee of "reliability," particularly in cases in which the music therapist and the researcher are the same person and his or her experiences are used as data, because it is unclear whether these experiences are shared by others or whether a repeated perception would evoke the same experience in the same person. The controlled subjectivity (mentioned in Chapter 2) proposed for this context, which entails the observer's being trained in the detection of countertransference, is a necessary precondition, but it is not sufficient to guarantee "reliability." We can strengthen "reliability" by involving several independent observers or by having the same observer repeat the same observation at different times. Observers can do this by repeatedly listening to one audiovisual recording and repeatedly reading through the notes they have made.

A further increase in "reliability" can be achieved by having a second independent researcher mentally reconstruct the chain of evidence at some later date. Therapists, who must record the chain of evidence in reports, are like detectives, who must precisely record the data on which their conclusions are based. A second researcher has to be able to check three things when reading these reports: the data selection ("reliability"), the data encoding ("construct validity"), and the suggested link between treatment and progress ("internal validity"). This method involves making four types of reports:

- The research proposal, which includes the definition of the problem and the procedure to be followed
- The rough data
- The processed data, which show the chain of evidence
- The final report, which takes the form of an article; because an article gives only a condensed representation of the course of the research and does not offer an opportunity to consider alternative possibilities, the processed database of the research project should be made accessible, within the bounds of the ethics code

"Construct Validity"

If we use a hypothesis as a starting point, then it is essential that we define the constructs in the hypothesis precisely. For example, what does *the client is relaxed* mean? How is this relaxed state manifested and how is the degree of relaxation measured? If we do not use existing constructs as a starting point but instead allow the constructs to emerge from the data, then we can use several different sources of constructs. In Chapter 2, we discussed the principle of *triangulation*, which entails the use of several observers, various techniques of collecting data (observation, interviews), or diverse theoretical models. Triangulation improves "reliability" and allows phenomena to be highlighted in a variety of ways and therefore to be labeled differently. It is consequently possible to check whether the phenomena are verbally represented as adequately as possible.

In grounded theory (Glaser and Strauss, 1967; Strauss and Corbin, 1990), we deliberately leave constructs "open" when answering the question "What is happening here?" We constantly adapt both the description and the naming of phenomena until they fit the event as well as possible. After we make the first selection of constructs, they function as sensitizing concepts that direct our searching process.

We strengthen the "construct validity" first of all by describing and naming the musical processes as intersubjectively as possible and subsequently linking them to existing psycho-pathological or psychotherapeutic constructs (Maso, 1989). This requires that we carefully consider whether a link to existing constructs is possible at all. The musical process and the existing psychopathological or psychotherapeutic constructs must fit together as adequately as possible. We must continually consider related constructs.

"Internal Validity"

The least therapists can do as far as "internal validity" is concerned is to register events that occur concurrently with therapy (changes in the situation at home, in other treatment, in weather conditions, in hobbies, in relationships, and so forth). There are also several specific methodological techniques, however, that we can use to verify "internal validity."

Pattern matching (see Chapter 2) is adequate for checking "internal validity." Despite the fact that phenomenologically speaking, every client, every therapist, every intervention, and every moment is unique and therefore impossible to replicate (Aldridge, 1993; Giorgi, 1985; Tüpker, 1990b), there are many similarities between members of each these categories. The use of multiple-case studies (Hutjes and van Buuren, 1992; Miles and Huberman, 1984) whenever practicable is therefore highly recommended. Multiple-case studies, which make use of parallel cases in which the start of treatment is staggered, can be used for treatment replication. Other methods that we can use to check "internal validity" are time-series analysis, disciplined subjectivity, peer debriefing, and member checking.

"External Validity"

Case-study research is not based on a representative sample of the population, so the results are essentially "valid" only for that one case. This is an oversimplification, however. After all, a single case can represent other similar cases; it is then known as a "typical" case. In a multiple-case study design, we can select the individual cases in order to discover whether similar cases show similar patterns and differing cases different patterns (Hutjes and van Buuren, 1992).

We can apply a music therapy treatment for depression, developed on the basis of case-study research, to new depressed clients. In "typical" cases, we will see to similar results. If we use that method to treat a schizophrenic client, then it will be unsuitable, at least in the same form. If we find that the method is equally applicable in both kinds of cases, then it is too general and has too little relevance for specific problems.

Conclusion

As far as research is concerned, music therapy is in an awkward position. Now that the inadequacies of quantitative experimental group research models are becoming apparent within the world of established psychotherapy research, music therapy researchers are more willing to consider qualitative single-case research. Because the scientific tradition within music therapy is still relatively new, however, music therapy as a field is in danger of both skipping stages in its scientific development and reverting to outdated positions.

We should acknowledge that quantitative research is a real possibility that is sometimes appropriate. It is incorrect to assume that "new paradigm" research is completely new. In fact, it can hardly be called a new paradigm at all, because for years, the phenomenological method dominated European psychology. It was superseded in Europe by experimental and statistical methods because these seemed to comply better with criteria that were considered important. This meant that because a methodological approach that was found to be relatively robust was declared universally applicable, the object of study was often rendered subordinate to the method. Such movements as humanistic psychology, however, began to emphasize human experience, and the accepted methodology was once again questioned. After all, neither human experience nor the therapeutic process is standard, average, or isolated.

A struggle now seems to have erupted between quantitative and qualitative researchers, but is this really an either-or situation? Are the two methods really comparable? A quantitative method can answer different questions than can a qualitative one. We should incorporate both methods into music therapy research in such a way that the chosen method of research depends on the question and the object to be studied, rather than the other way around. A research method is a means, not an end.

A COMMON GROUND FOR
RESEARCH CRITERIA?

For me, one of the most important experiences during the 1994 Düsseldorf Symposium for Qualitative Research and its follow-up meetings was the discussion about "criteria," "rules," and "guidelines" in qualitative research. Most researchers at the symposium argued that qualitative research needs its own criteria because it starts from a very different paradigm, with its own conceptions of reality and the gathering of knowledge, that rejects generalization, causality, and "objectivity." Because I felt their way of doing research did not essentially differ from the way I do it, I asked myself why I can still use traditional criteria without experiencing cognitive dissonance. It became clear to me that I use traditional concepts to describe new qualitative procedures; other qualitative researchers in the Netherlands also do it that way. I was not satisfied, however, by telling myself that I was justified because I do what some people in the Netherlands do, so I asked myself whether as a qualitative researcher I attached to preconscious quantitative thoughts. This section of the chapter is an expression of my search into why I believe the old concepts can be used when talking about new contents.

Since Lincoln and Guba (1982, 1985) introduced the concept of trustworthiness, qualitative researchers have seemed to be astonished when in the context of qualitative research such concepts as "internal validity," "external validity", "reliability," and "objectivity" are used. In the conventional paradigm, these four concepts were identified with such techniques as experimental design, representative sampling, test-retest replication, averaged intersubjective agreement, and standardized testing. Because these procedures differ fundamentally from the basic axioms of qualitative research, that astonishment is understandable. If, as a qualitative researcher, you are convinced that there is no fragmentable reality and there are no simple causal relationships, then using an experimental and control group to study the influence of an independent on a dependent variable makes no sense to you. If you think statements free from time and context are impossible, you will argue that realities can be neither generalized, replicated, nor understood by a noninteracting inquirer. You will find sampling, repeated testing, and standardized scales useless. In qualitative research, there are no "variables," "effects," "control" and "experimental" groups, or "measurements."

Lincoln and Guba reject the concepts of "internal validity," "external validity," "reliability," and "objectivity" because they believe these concepts to be inconsistent with qualitative inquiry. What many seem to have forgotten, however, is that Lincoln and Guba stress the fact that for the quantitative and qualitative researcher, the same four methodological questions are appropriate (Lincoln and Guba, 1985):

- What is the "truth" of an inquiry's findings for the respondents?
- To what degree are these findings applicable in other contexts?
- Would the findings be consistently repeated if the inquiry were replicated?
- To what degree do the findings stem from the characteristics of the respondents and not from biases of the inquirer?

To me, it seems that the concepts of "internal validity," "external validity," "reliability," and "objectivity" are similar to these fundamental questions. The difficulty is that in quantitative research, these concepts are defined in a very reductionistic way and are identified with the procedures of experimentation, sampling, replication, and instrumentation. Lincoln and Guba use the concepts in exactly the same reductionistic and operationalized way quantitative researchers do. In my opinion, however, these concepts can be still of value in qualitative research if they are described in another way and linked to procedures that fit the qualitative axioms. Aldridge (1996a) also sticks to "validity" when talking about qualitative research. He returns to the ". . . archaic meaning of the word": a strong, robust argument. He writes that "validity as trustworthiness" means ". . . to show that the work is well grounded, to make transparent the premises that are being used, to develop a set of sound interpretations and relevant observations, and to make these interpretations credible."

Of course, you may ask why we should retain these concepts. I answer you with a personal argument and arguments about parsimony and ease of communication. From the very first time I contemplated qualitative research, it was clear to me that these concepts needed different contents, but I never thought it impossible to use them. Also, introducing new concepts to address the same questions seems to me like raising barriers to hinder communication.

We are confronted with the same issue when communicating about music therapy in general. Should we completely develop our own music therapy language, or should we only integrate those of our concepts that can be understood by different disciplines? For instance, do we need our own theories of music therapy psychopathology and psychotherapy, or should we demonstrate that mental disorders, as described by other disciplines, are expressed through musical experiences and that music therapy is a collection of musical processes that trigger psychotherapeutic processes that in turn can help to heal mental disorders? I think we need to link the language of music therapy with the language of other helping professions.

The same holds for qualitative research. We need a common ground that facilitates communication between quantitative and qualitative researchers. I am not saying that in essence these types of research are the same. They are ". . . mutually exclusive ways of thinking about the world . . . and cannot be adopted at the same time . . ." (Bruscia, 1995a). But even when we respect the fundamental differences, we still can ask if there are some shared methodological lines of inquiry. When—like Lincoln and Guba point out—there is, we can ask if it would be fruitful to use a language that indicates that these questions are shared. What we need to ask next is when and why a quantitative versus a qualitative paradigm is indicated to answer these questions. Which approach we should use depends on the type of answers we want to give (the purpose of the study) and the attributes of the phenomena under study. I am aware that this looks like some sort of a dilemma because using conventional concepts carries the risk that we lose the fundamental axioms of the qualitative paradigm.

It should be possible, however, both to use conventional concepts to facilitate communication between researchers and to respect the fundamental axioms of qualitative research by adjusting their content.

Let us take a closer look at the new concepts introduced by Lincoln and Guba and try to understand what they mean.

Credibility

Credibility (instead of "internal validity") means testing whether the reconstructions made by researchers are credible to the constructors of the original multiple realities. Instead of describing the causal links between fragments of reality, researchers describe complex mutual shapings, interrelationships between multiple aspects of reality. Here, everything influences everything else and each element interacts with all of the others. There is no directionality; events simply happen.

The procedures researchers use to increase the probability of obtaining credible findings show that they try, for instance, to prevent distortions, selectivity, and biases. Researchers want to identify relevant characteristics, those things that really count. This interest resembles that of experimental researchers, who want to know which variables really count. Furthermore, qualitative researchers may investigate the process of "enabling," which means introducing elements in the context that do not cause changes but make them possible. (The word *element* is used by Lincoln and Guba.) Even if there is no causal link, you might argue that there is some sort of an "effect" here.

If we look into the goals of qualitative research that Bruscia (1995a) discusses, we find "analysis," meaning the discovery of patterns, recurrences, categories, types. When, in the way Bruscia illustrates analysis, researchers look, for instance, at relationships between nonverbal and musical events, changes in behavior before versus after treatment, and relationships between verbal expressions of experiences and musical improvisations, then this is no linear causality. This interest in connections between events, experiences, materials, and personal characteristics, however—this process of linking up—is like the search for connections in quantitative research. Although their conceptions of reality differ, qualitative and quantitative researchers seem to share the same intention when looking for connections.

Aigen's statement (1996a) that he selects only those incidents that support his interpretations could be misunderstood. There always should be verification of whether researchers' interpretations are grounded in data, and the chains of evidence researchers construct should be examined. If these things are not done, findings reflect only the personal views of the researchers and not the multiple perspectives of the participants. Because in qualitative research there is no belief in an independent reality "out there," connections made by researchers are not verified or falsified by "reality"; they are instead seen as "reconstructions" that have to make sense for those who made the constructions in the first place. We could say the reconstructed patterns need to be sound, well-grounded, and "valid" as experienced by the participants.

Finally, I must mention a seemingly paradoxical point. In qualitative research, when "causality" is rejected and yet credibility is ensured by interaction with participants, then perhaps we must after all concede the need for causality. Human beings— therapists and clients—construct their realities in terms of causal relationships.

Transferability

Transferability (instead of "external validity") addresses the question of whether what is researched in one context can be used in another. Because a context is not a "sample" and every context is different, we cannot generalize findings. Only when there is a degree of similarity between the original and new context can we transfer the results of research; therefore, qualitative researchers must provide a multilayered description of the original context. Although qualitative researchers' basic axioms about reality and the procedures they use to determine applicability differ fundamentally from quantitative researchers' procedures of sampling and generalization, I believe the concept of "external validity" translates as the grounding of findings in another context.

Because qualitative researchers point out that there is no stability, qualitative researchers do not strive to repeat a similar inquiry process in the "same unit." When we think holistically, there is no similar situation in which one experience can be replicated in exactly the same way. Not only do human contexts change, but so does the interaction between researcher and participants; thus, in qualitative research, the design will never be the same. It is impossible to repeat what is a more or less unique process.

Dependability

Instead of "reliability," the concept of *dependability* was introduced to take into account these factors of instability. It seems to me that by using this new concept, we win something, but we lose something, too. While it is not possible to repeat history, it still is possible to repeat *looking* at it. A researcher can experience different thoughts, feelings, or images about the same event at different times, as can both participants and observers. Doing research requires some sort of "replication" within and between human minds. The outcome is not "the truth" but a set of "multiple perspectives." Thus, "replication" is possible in qualitative research: it is not replication of the unique treatment but a replication of the descriptions of this uniqueness. There will emerge a never-ending field of stories (Kenny, 1996a).

By using prolonged engagement, qualitative researchers try to prevent distortions, selectivity, and biases. They also try to identify the most characteristic elements. Lincoln and Guba (1985) mention "testing for misinformation," which is done through the use of repeated observations and of multiple perspectives from different participants. I believe that such concepts as "intrareliability" and "interreliability" can be used to name these qualitative procedures.

Confirmability

Qualitative researchers argue that there can be no "objectivity" because there is no "objective reality" and no "truth." They see realities as subjective constructed entities. Using the human instrument instead of standardized test ensures that in researchers' reconstructions, changing contexts, the meaning of these contexts, and the subjective perspectives of the participants will be included. No context loaded with subjectivities can be understood without a researcher who, because of his or her own personal experiences, tries to be open and empathic to these subjectivities.

Because "objectivity" in quantitative research has been reduced to the average experience of a number of individuals and/or findings on standardized tests, qualitative researchers have replaced it with "confirmability." Lincoln and Guba (1985) conclude that the issue is no longer the investigator's characteristics but the characteristics of the data. When the authors deem it important that findings are confirmed by data and when inquirer bias about that data is investigated by peer debriefing and auditing, however, this interest resembles the wish for "objectivity." We must be aware of the possibility that data are biased by ideas, feelings, theories, and concepts that merely reflect the researcher's preconceptions.

RULES AND GUIDELINES IN QUALITATIVE RESEARCH

With the help of rules, a quantitative researcher knows from the beginning how to proceed. The hypothesis, instrumentation, and design are developed before research starts and there are no changes during the research process. In several types of qualitative research, however, there is an "emergent design," which implies that there is no hypothesis, there are no measuring instruments, and there is no fixed design at the start. If there were, the essence of these types of qualitative research would be lost because they are characterized by interaction between inquirer and context of inquiry. If there is interaction, there will be change.

Qualitative music therapy researchers often categorically deny that there are rules in qualitative research. I ask, though, what do we mean by a rule? How do we define the word *rule*? Is it—as are the concepts of "validity" and "reliability"—defined in the conventional way? Then the word *guideline,* which I introduced in my own qualitative research as outcome, would be better. A guideline *can* be used, but we are not *obliged* to use it. There is a difference, however, if we interpret a "rule" as a prerequisite that ensures that what we are doing is indeed research and not clinical practice. One of the dangers of the qualitative research paradigm is that sometimes everything seems to be research, but as Bruscia (1996a) points out, "research is not writing about one's clinical work, making up one's own theory, or sharing one's personal views." If these differences exist, we need "rules" so we can be sure what is research and what is not. Using subjectivity incorrectly can disguise poor scholarship; so can doing away with rules. There *are* rules in qualitative research, and denying this is inauthentic (Bruscia, 1996a). Of course, not every available technique or method for meeting the criteria of "internal validity" (credibility), "external validity" (transferability), "reliability" (dependability), and "objectivity" (confirmability) is used every time. Here, the freedom to choose is expressed by the concept of "guidelines." Whatever technique or method we use, we nevertheless need such "rules" as "openness," "interaction," and "dialectics" to ensure that we are doing qualitative research.

THE MUSIC THERAPIST AS RESEARCHER

One of the justifications for interaction is that of Lincoln and Guba (1985), who state that meaningful research is impossible without the full understanding and cooperation of the respondents. Bruscia (1996a) says that qualitative research improves when the researcher is the subject's therapist or when the researcher interacts with the subject. The interaction between researcher and context is part of the qualitative paradigm. Because in therapy the therapist is the one who interacts most closely with the client, the roles of therapist and researcher can be filled by the same person. In discussing research he has conducted in his own clinical practice, Aigen (1996a) asks whether research should be done while treatment is in progress. I agree with him that combining treatment and research can be of benefit for the client.

When the therapist and the researcher are the same person, a problem does arise—authenticity (Bruscia, 1996a). Being a therapist is not the same as being a researcher. In therapy, the therapist seeks insight for the client's sake, not for the sake of other clients. There can be inauthenticity when we are not aware of our own perspectives. How do we achieve authenticity methodologically? Because I believe it is very difficult to slip forth and back from one of the roles to the other, it is much more easy and authentic when there are two people fill these roles: one is the therapist and the other is the researcher. Then, we minimize inauthenticity. Bruscia's suggestion that the therapist/researcher is, in an intrasubjective way, responsible for the authenticity of intent to me seems an insufficient criterion. We know that the awareness of our intent often is distorted. It is possible that a therapist can fully know this and be able to move between these different roles, but it is a characteristic of research that these processes must be verified.

QUALITATIVE OR QUANTITATIVE RESEARCH?

The question whether only qualitative or quantitative research should be used gives way to several perspectives. Several therapists who have tried to describe their personal therapeutic practice by means of quantitative research have come to the conclusion that it was impossible to do so. Other researchers hold the position that we can do both types of research because there are different types of research questions and data.

In music therapy research, too, both perspectives are possible. On one hand, we could argue that only qualitative research should be used because the goals of music therapy research are incompatible with quantitative research. For instance, if these goals are "wholeness," "process," "essence," and "subjective experience," then indeed quantitative research is unsuitable. On the other hand, we could say that quantitative and qualitative research are complementary. If we think it is important to research effects as well as processes, then quantitative research is the right method for studying the former, and qualitative research, the latter. I am fully aware that this distinction is based on my personal perspective. Several qualitative researchers differ, saying that there cannot be a division between "process" and "effect" because in their scientific paradigm, "effects" do not exist. They would tell me that I am not a genuine qualitative researcher. I would answer that qualitative research has many faces, that there are gradations between the "new" qualitative scientific paradigm and the "old" quantitative paradigm. I am somewhere in between.

For music therapists, "process" research is most often believed to be as important or more important than "effect" research. Music therapists are interested in the process of experience between the start and the end of therapy. It is also true that "effects" are part of the process. Quantitative effect research, however, can tell us something about music therapy, too. When there is a difference between beginning and ending scores on standardized tests, then this is "something." In other words, quantitative research tells us "something" about music therapy. It does not give us the "essence," and we should remember that the "something" is not the "whole"—but it *is* "something." We should not put it aside because it is not the whole.

CONCLUSION

Qualitative and quantitative research share some fundamental methodological questions. The concepts that address these questions can be the same, but the answers to these questions differ fundamentally because of different paradigms. Qualitative researchers want to identify relevant characteristics, discover patterns, and study the process of enabling. The chain of evidence resulting from this needs to be "internally valid" as experienced by the participants in their unique context. It is also possible that the findings can be "externally valid," which means that they may be of help in another context. Because a qualitative researcher uses prolonged engagement, repeated descriptions, and multiple perspectives, "intrareliability" and "interreliability" prevent distortions and selectivity. Peer debriefing and auditing guard against inquirer biases and guarantee "objectivity."

In qualitative research, some "rules" provide the sense that the activity is "research" and not clinical work or theory. "Rules" also guarantee that the research is "qualitative." "Guidelines" are methodological possibilities. Because qualitative researchers are free to use them or not, research can develop out of the unique context and unique interaction. The music therapist can act as a researcher, and it is important that the experience of the music therapist is part of the research. Because of the need for authenticity, however, it is preferable to use a research team, where the roles of music therapist and researcher are filled by two different people.

The following lists (modified from Smeijsters, 1996c, with permission) summarize the issues discussed in this chapter.

We must ask the following basic research questions:
- Which phenomena seem to be important over time?
- How do we encode these phenomena?
- How do we connect these phenomena in patterns?
- For whom do these phenomena and patterns seem to have meaning?
- Which phenomena and patterns seem to be important at other times and places?

We need procedures:
- For selecting the most important data
- For encoding these data and giving meaning to them
- For reconstructing patterns in the data
- For excluding personal bias
- For exploring the universality of findings

We can integrate old and new concepts of research as follows:
- Reliability/dependability: replicating descriptions of uniqueness
- Internal validity/credibility: making reconstructed patterns credible for participants

- Objectivity/confirmability: grounding researchers' subjective impressions in the subjective multiple experiences of the participants
- External validity/transferability: exploring the usefulness of findings in another context

Old concepts and basic research questions in qualitative research:
- "Reliability": What is replicated in multiple descriptions over time?
- "Construct validity": Which (new) words are used to encode the multiple descriptions of one phenomenon?
- "Internal validity": Which credible patterns between phenomena can be constructed?
- "Objectivity": Are descriptions, codes, and patterns grounded in the subjective experiences of the participants?
- "External validity": Which findings are transferable to other times and places?

Quantitative research can be contrasted with qualitative research as follows:

Quantitative	**Qualitative**
• Universal theory independent of context	• Naturalistic local theory generated from context
• Linear causality of isolated selected variables	• Dependency of complex inter-related phenomena
• Experimental manipulation and limited change	• Ongoing process of change
• Standardized measurement (using the same items everywhere)	• Researcher as research instrument, being "open" to experience
• Objectivity as nonsubjectivity	• Grounding of researcher's subjectivity in participants' experiences
• Replication of events	• Replication of personal perspectives

In qualitative procedures, researchers:
- Use reports of participants (member checking)
- Ask independent observers to make observations and interview experts (peer debriefing)
- Repeat their own observations and analyze them

- Generate and adjust hypotheses
- Construct patterns and sequences
- Use several sources, data-collecting techniques, and theoretical models (triangulation)
- Construct a chain of evidence
- Ask independent researchers to check the constructed chain of evidence
- Stimulate independent researchers to execute similar qualitative research studies to explore guidelines (multiple-case studies)

Part II

EXAMPLES OF QUALITATIVE RESEARCH IN MUSIC THERAPY

Chapter 4

THE SEARCH FOR MEANING AND RELEVANCE: PHENOMENOLOGY

GENERAL PRINCIPLES

In Europe, the phenomenological tradition in psychotherapy is very rich. Since the late 1980s, phenomenology has received strong attention in qualitative music therapy research in the United States. This chapter therefore concentrates on developments in the United States.

Forinash (1995) wrote an excellent overview of phenomenological research in music therapy; this chapter does not give her descriptions in full here but does summarize her definition of *phenomenology*. Forinash and Gonzalez (1989) point out that quantitative methods ". . . miss the very essence of what we experience as music therapy clinicians". In that sentence, three concepts are combined: *essence, experience,* and *clinician.* If we put the accent on *essence,* then the sentence reads as if quantitative research completely misses the point, failing to uncover the essence of music therapy. When we stress *experience* and *clinician,* however, the interpretation is different: it appears that clinical music therapists experience music therapy in a way not reflected by quantitative research. Implicit in this statement is that research should take into account the music therapist's experience. Already, this is an *a priori* phenomenological statement. What we are then saying is: "Because music therapy research needs to be phenomenological, it should be qualitative (that is, phenomenological)." You may think I am kidding, but I only want to point out the value-bound origin of this seemingly straightforward statement. Of course the experiences of music therapists are important, but studying these experiences is just one way of doing research. Can doing so make clear for us "the" essence of music therapy, or just the way music therapists experience its essence?

Phenomenology is a research method that unfolds events the way they are experienced by people and describes the essential qualities of this experience. "The" reality is not important; instead, the way reality is perceived, how it becomes a phenomenon in the person, is the focus. Meaning and relevance, not truth, are sought. Phenomenological researchers do not test hypotheses; they give descriptions. They make use of phenomenological reduction: they take a phenomenon as it appears to them, without attempting to uncover an "objective" reality behind the appearance, and are open-minded and suspend previous knowledge and opinions (bracketing, epoché). They also uses eidetic reduction (imaginative variation): exchanging subtracting or adding characteristics of the phenomenon to see if the essence changes.

To me, one of the most difficult points in phenomenology is the exclusion of previous knowledge. Who among us can be sure that our emotions, sensations, and associations are grounded in the experience we are studying and not in our own individual personalities? This brings up a difference between phenomenology and other qualitative research methods: researchers who say that there are multiple perspectives do not believe that their experiences of who they are as people can be fully ignored. Phenomenologists, however, seem to believe that this is possible and that there can be some standardized "phenomenologically reduced human instrument" that can give us the "essence of the experience of a phenomenon." Ruud's remark (1996a) that the phenomenologist makes ". . . naive assumptions about the possibility of defining essences, of seeing things as they really are . . ." is close to my opinion. Forinash (1995), referring to Sartre, writes that the phenomenologist realizes that there are multiple perspectives, however, and that the phenomenon can be studied only as it appears to the one perceiving it. This is, of course, in line with qualitative researchers who take a constructivistic stand.

Tesch (1992) sees Paul Colaizzi, William Fischer, Rolf von Eckartsberg, Adrian van Kaam, and Amadeo Giorgi as the formulators of phenomenological methodology in psychology, in which researchers try to determine "necessary and sufficient constituents" of a phenomenon. Specific views of some of these authors are discussed later in this chapter.

METHODS

Colaizzi (1978) distinguishes between reflexive and empirical forms of phenomenology. *Reflexive* means that researchers use their own experiences as data. This form can be heuristic when there is a meditative and intuitive process of inner searching for deeper awareness. In phenomenological reflection, researchers use reflective thinking to discover meaning. These methods come close to the qualitative principle of researchers serving as instruments. *Empirical* means that descriptive protocols from other subjects are used. In protocol analysis, transcripts (protocols) of interviews or self-reports are analyzed by means of several steps:

1. Reading all descriptions
2. Extracting significant statements in each protocol
3. Formulating what participants mean in these statements (formulated meanings)
4. Clustering overlapping formulated meanings from different protocols and organizing these in themes
5. Validating these themes by returning to the original protocol
6. Writing an exhaustive description of the topic under study
7. Making a statement of its fundamental structure
8. Validating the description by research participants

These research steps are also used in Colaizzi's method of imaginative listening. The difference is that the researcher uses a dialogical interview with the participant.

A third type of empirical phenomenology is perceptual description, in which the researcher observes events that are difficult to communicate or conceptualize, by means of primitive perception, without already developed cognitive constructs. This is important for music therapists, who often claim that experiences in music can neither be described by normal consciousness nor communicated. Colaizzi's distinction between reflexive and empirical phenomenology has been criticized by some because of the dualism of personal experience and others' experiences. Other phenomenologists stress the fact that every phenomenologist reflects his or her own experiences when trying to give meaning to experiences of other subjects.

Tesch (1992) summarizes the different methods that have arisen from the use of perceptual description. The first is dialogical phenomenology, introduced by Stephan Strasser and used by Fischer. With this method, phenomenologists use "internal dialogues" to develop multiple descriptions of personal experience that then are used in dialogues with others about their experiences of the same phenomenon (the "external dialogue"). This method comes close to the qualitative principle of multiple perspectives.

Eckartsberg has developed another type of dialogical phenomenology in which researcher and participant cooperate closely to make sense of the participant's self-reports. Both partners influence each other's understanding; both change and experience personal growth. My own research, developed at the Music Therapy Laboratory of Hogeschool van Arnhem (Nijmegen, The Netherlands), is characterized by dialogues between researcher and music therapist. Not only do personal perspectives develop reciprocally, but this development is also of direct benefit to the client. Of course, the aspect of the researcher's self-development raises questions of both ethics and authenticity. The researcher or music therapist should not seek self-development: therapy is directed at helping the client, not the therapist.

John Heron and James Barrell introduced an experiential method, in which the distinction between researcher and subject fades further. Here, researchers are not the ones describing the "necessary and sufficient constituents" of a phenomenon, nor is there a dialogue with the subjects. On the contrary, researchers instruct the participants to describe the "necessary and sufficient constituents" of a phenomenon themselves. Thus, participants themselves become researchers.

EXAMPLES OF PHENOMENOLOGICAL RESEARCH IN MUSIC THERAPY

Forinash (1995) defines the key difference between quantitative research and phenomenology as ". . . trying to prove whether music therapy intervention works and trying to understand what meaning (personal, societal, etc.) the music therapy intervention has for those who experience it."

In this section, let us focus on two examples of phenomenological research by Forinash, one belonging to the categories of perceptual description and phenomenological reflection and the other to the category of imaginative listening. As mentioned above, the researcher using perceptual description observes events that are difficult to communicate or conceptualize by means of primitive perception, while the researcher using phenomenological reflection employs reflective thinking to discover meaning. In a case described by Forinash and Gonzalez (1989), there is an event that is difficult to describe: music therapy with a woman who dies during the session.

The research steps in this case are based on Ferrara's work (1984). I quote elements of the case to illustrate the steps.

1. **Compile Data on the Client's Background:** Collect information about the psychosocial history of the client and his or her family.

   > Sara was 42 years old . . . with a diagnosis of breast cancer with metastasis to the brain. . . . She . . . had received chemotherapy treatments. Sara was married and had two children. . . . Her husband had been an alcoholic . . . and committed suicide. . . .
   >
   > Sara was referred to music therapy on this particular day because death was expected to occur within hours. . . .

2. **Describe the Session:** Describe the actual music therapy session. Make a transcript of the audiovisual tape. Are songs being sung? Is there improvisation? How is the music therapist behaving? How is the client behaving?

   > Aimee-Sawyer and I [Michele Forinash] entered Sara's single room. . . . She was lying in bed with oxygen tubing and was unresponsive, breathing in a very deep, jerky manner. The room

was somewhat dark. . . . The gray wintered day filtered through the blinds. . . .

We began to improvise on guitar and added our voices, harmonizing on "ooh" and "ah" sounds. . . . I said that I felt very confused and did not know what to do. I felt very lost. . . . I chose the song "Perhaps Love." . . . I next chose "Somewhere Over the Rainbow." . . . Aimee-Sawyer and I played and sang the lyrics of both songs, as well as vocalized on "ooh" and "ah." . . . Sara's breathing began to change. . . . Aimee-Sawyer suggested that we improvise a song with peaceful images and words. . . . Sara's breathing continued to change. The hard and sharp breaths became fewer, while the soft and gentle breaths became more frequent. I realized that Sara was dying. . . . I became very aware of my own heart beating. . . . I was afraid . . . I was filled with fear. . . . After a few minutes of silence, we began to improvise again . . . around major seventh chords. . . . Sara's breathing continued to change. . . . Her breathing had at first seemed like waves pounding on the shore. As time had passed, her breath had become soft and shallow. . . . I improvised, basing the rhythm on Sara's breathing. As her breaths became more shallow and slower, I changed to softer and slower music. . . . I was looking but no longer really "seeing." . . . I stopped playing. . . . Thoughts crossed my mind. "Does Sara need to die alone? Are we crowding her? Should we stay? Should we leave?" I finally turned and looked at Aimee-Sawyer. There was a tear running down her cheek. . . . Sara's breathing became more shallow. I knew she would soon die. I felt a connection with Sara in the music. Another image came to mind. It seemed that we had been united as an airplane is to the ground that it rests upon. . . . I said to myself, "God, reach out for this woman; she is coming to you." . . . Her breaths were more shallow and less frequent. I no longer followed her in the music; instead the music continued on its own. . . . She did not breathe again. . . .

3. **Study the Syntax:** Analyze the musical elements (pre-composed and improvisational music as well).

   In this section Forinash and Gonzalez give a precise analysis of the music:

   - Improvisation with chord progression: I–IV–V⁷–I in G major
   - "Perhaps Love": I–vi–ii⁷–V⁷ (×2), iii–vi–IV–V⁷, ii⁷–V⁷–I
   - "Somewhere Over the Rainbow": I–vii–iii–V⁷–IV–I, IV–iv–I–V⁷–I
   - An improvisation creating lyrics over structured instrumental music in I–IV–V⁷–I in G major, in waltz time, in a slow, rocking tempo; words reflected resting, relaxing, peacefulness, trust
   - An improvisation centered around two major seventh chords, Cmaj⁷ to Fmaj⁷; slower tempo, based on the rhythm of the client's breathing
   - Silence
   - The final improvisation in common time: I–ii⁷sus⁴–Imaj⁷–ii⁷sus⁴–I, progression in A major; Sara died during this improvisation

4. **Analyze Sound as Such:** Describe the qualities of the sounds. Add statements about the client's emotional, physical, and psychic states.

> The sound that was most present . . . was that of Sara's breathing. . . . Following her breathing throughout the session was a primary source of information on how she was changing during the session. She initially breathed in a hard and jerky manner, like deep sighs. This was followed by a gradual change to a softer sound of relaxed, easy breathing. . . . I was also very aware . . . of the soft hum of the oxygen machine. . . . Its sound served as a poignant reminder of the difference between humanity and machinery. The words as sounds in the session were also in my awareness. The "ooh" and "ah" sounds on which we vocalized seemed to fill the room at times and add a dimension to the air and space in the room. . . .

5. **Analyze Semantics:** Describe the referential meaning of the session. To what is the music is referring? What does it reflect? Which images arise?

> . . . The first image was that of an ocean. Sara's breathing seemed like waves retreating from the shore. . . . The second image was that of an airplane and its connection with the ground. . . . The third image . . . appeared when I said to myself, "God, reach out for this woman; she is coming to you. Open your arms and take her in." . . .

6. **Use Ontology:** Try to become aware of the "life world" clients bring to the session, the perspective and meaning from their world, their existential reality.

> It is not possible for me to describe Sara's life world. I cannot know what she was experiencing in this session. I can only intuit from what I knew about her history and what I sensed from her in the session. In doing this, I suspected that her transition from life to death was difficult, certainly sensed a holding on. . . .

7. **Do a Metacritical Evaluation:** Review the data collected in the previous steps.

> . . . In the auditory field, the relationship of Sara's breathing to the music was an essential aspect of the unfolding of this session. . . . The visual field contained not only what was physically present but also images that were triggered by the visual presence. . . . The experience presented here is that of the therapist. . . . I can offer no far-reaching conclusions about the nature of music therapy.

The most impressive aspect of this process, I think, is the way the music therapist expresses her deep feelings and those of her colleague. She is able to describe in feelings, thoughts, images, visual and auditory perceptions, and body sensations a most impressive existential life event, being close to a person who moves from life into death. She succeeded very well in taking the reader through her experience, in communicating subjective experience to let the reader feel what she felt. Every time I read what she has written about this case, I am moved to tears.

I am not as convinced about the usefulness of the step involving syntax. For several reasons, I think it is a strange bird, as if music therapists feel obliged to always say something about musical structure. Is it so important to write down chord progressions? Of course the music therapist needs to know how to play songs, but does this information add something to phenomenological understanding? By the presence of their description, we infer that these particular chord progressions are very important, but are they? What is much more important is the emotional content of these songs. Is it phenomenology when we use an already existing method of musical analysis? In fact, we are then using musical preconceptions. What is more, there is no experience to be found in the chord progressions. I believe traditional musical analysis reduces music to technical ingredients and cannot give us any phenomenological meaning. Another important point is—as the authors themselves note—that this research is about music therapists' experiences, not clients' experiences. This type of research has been used also by Amir (1990).

In the second example of phenomenological research below, imaginative listening has been used: these are open-ended interviews about clinical improvisation with music therapists from the Nordoff-Robbins Music Therapy Clinic at New York University. The music therapists selected one videotaped session and reviewed it with the researcher, and the researcher asked questions. Each interview was transcribed and the transcripts were analyzed.

Forinash made use of research steps developed by Giorgi (1984, 1985). These steps are described and illustrated with examples from her research. The natural context of the phenomenon and the researcher's perspective are both very important.

1. **Find a Sense of the Whole:** Read the text, try to understand the language of the describer, and get a sense of the whole. Use multiple readings when there are many pages.

2. **Define Meaning Units:** The text has to be broken down
    in meaning units to make it manageable.

    What makes a unit a meaning unit? Giorgi de-
    scribes it as follows: ". . . [a unit discrimination can be
    made] whenever the researcher, upon reading the text, be-
    comes aware of a change of meaning of the situation for
    the subject that appears to be psychological sensitive."
    When, for instance, the music therapist shifts from what
    his or her intentions were during the session to how the
    client reacted musically, a discrimination between two
    units can be made. It is important to mention that these
    discriminations are made spontaneously.
    Giorgi points out that the difference from tradi-
    tional content analysis is that the phenomenological
    method is not mechanical, quantitative, or limited to
    manifest content. He also stresses that the way meaning
    units are made depends on the researcher's perspective.

3. **Transform the Material into Psychological Lan-
    guage:** Giorgi uses a process of reflection and imaginative
    variation. The researcher tries to arrive at a general cate-
    gory by going through concrete expressions. Psychological
    language is meant to elucidate the truly essential.

    Let me give an example of imaginative variation.
    Say, for instance, as in Giorgi's example (1985), a father
    gives his own chess set to his son and it turns out that the
    son uses the chess set not the way the father intended but
    takes out the weights in the chess pieces. "Is it important
    to mention that it is a chess set?" Giorgi asks himself. He
    changes the word *chess* to *gift* and concludes that this does
    not change the essential psychological meaning. This
    transformation from *chess* to *gift* is a transformation in
    psychological reality: the concrete event is transformed
    into a "gift transaction." Other examples are: the re-
    searcher's transforming the fact that it was the father's
    own chess set into "a gift with deep personal significance,"
    or the father's observation that his son was excited and to
    him seemed to sense its symbolic value into "father per-
    ceives his son as apparently receiving and using the gift as

intended." The psychological language deals with perceptions and intentions.

4. **Synthesize the Transformed Meaning Units:** The researcher synthesizes and integrates the insights from all transformed meaning units, then makes a consistent description of the psychological structure of the event. Finally, the researcher communicates the structure to other researchers for criticism. This resembles peer debriefing.

Using these research steps, Forinash found 12 meaning units that show how music therapists from the Nordoff-Robbins orientation experience clinical improvisation. To me, it is not clear which rationale she used to extract the meaning units. There are several possibilities. One might choose only those units found in each interview, but as Giorgi (1985) states, a meaning unit can be based on only one subject. With each meaning unit, Forinash gives a quotient, writing that the meaning unit has been found in "three of eight therapists and both co-directors (1), five of eight and both co-directors (2), six of eight and both co-directors (3), three of eight and both co-directors (4), five of eight and one co-director (5), four of eight and one co-director (6), all of eight and both co-directors (7), five of eight and both co-directors (8), all of eight and both co-directors (9), frequences missing (1), all of eight and both co-directors (11), all of eight and both co-directors (12)."

There seems to be a hidden quantitative criterion in this: there should be at least five people who share the same meaning unit, and there should be at least one of the co-directors in this group. If there is a quantified intersubjectivity, however, then four of the meaning units seem to be most important. Meaning units 7, 9, 11 and 12, listed below in bold italics, are shared by all music therapists and both co-directors:

1. **Natural Ability:** Music therapists experience themselves as having some natural ability to express themselves in music and to relate to people.
2. **Musical Biography:** Music therapists find their own musical background has been important.
3. **The Unknown:** Music therapists experience improvisation as facing the unknown, a mystery, without formula.

4. **Vulnerability:** Music therapists feel that defenses are stripped away, that it is impossible to hide.
5. **Pressure:** Music therapists feel stressed because every session is videotaped and analyzed.
6. **Difficulty in Defining:** Music therapists find it difficult to put the experience of improvisation into words.
7. *Spontaneity, Creativity, Intuition:* Music therapists experience moments where they freely respond, develop and expand their own and their client's responses, and proceed without any apparent external reason.
8. **Interplay of Intuition and Rationality:** Music therapists experience a shift from an instinctive start to a more conscious way of working or the other way around.
9. *Rational, Conscious Choice:* Music therapists describe moments where rational conscious choices are made.
10. **Self:** Postsession analysis gives insight into music therapists' personal feelings and issues.
11. *Music:* Using postsession analysis, music therapists gain insight into their individual relationships to music.
12. *The Child:* Music therapists experience an awareness and learning in relationship to the child in the session.

Meaning units 7, 8, 9 are very close. It would be interesting to know how they interact. As her final step, Forinash used member checking in stead of peer debriefing: she submitted the results to the music therapists who had been interviewed. She reports that almost all music therapists wanted to refine their initial words. What does this mean? I think it shows how difficult it is to translate experiences into words. Experiences are much deeper than can ever be put into words. This also highlights the need for musical improvisation that enables expression of the unspeakable.

Chapter 5

GROUNDED THEORY

GENERAL PRINCIPLES

In grounded theory, introduced by Glaser and Strauss (1967) and further developed by Strauss and Corbin (1990), conceptualizing is central. The goal of this research method is the development of interrelated concepts that can describe reality as well as possible. Reality is not described by means of an already existing theory and hypotheses that are deduced from it. Instead, theories and hypotheses are generated from reality and become "grounded" in reality. Although the proponents of every theory claim that their theories are grounded in reality, there is a difference in grounded theory. In quantitative research, we suppose there to be a universal theory that we can apply to different contexts and from which we can deduce hypotheses that also fit another specific context. In grounded theory, however, we create an ideographic theory that fits one specific context. *Grounded theory* to some extent resembles phenomenological reduction, in which existing theories are excluded and the phenomena are described without preconceptions.

Before discussing the research steps, we must understand the types of research notes:

1. **Data:** These can be self-reports, interviews, tapes, observation data, minutes of a team discussion, and so on. Researchers often make short summaries out of these raw data.

2. **Concepts in Progress:** Researchers can select, shorten or extend passages from the raw data with other passages

and code them by concept. This way, they develop a "concept card" with a concept as title and a short description of the concept as definition. They continuously adjust concepts and descriptions by iterative exchange with the data until there are enough concept cards to give an optimal reflection of the data. They use the relevance of the concepts as an criterion. With these concepts, they organize the raw data by making classifications, abstracting, and interpreting.

3. **Memos:** Memos note the ideas and questions of the research process, reflecting the researcher's argumentation and stimulating him or her to reflect on the course of research. They also make it possible for an independent researcher to replicate the chain of evidence. An independent researcher can determine whether, in the light of the raw data, the original researcher developed the right concepts and made the right classifications, abstractions, and interpretations.

Research steps are discussed below.

Exploration

Exploration involves:

1. Registration of data—for instance, by writing down the event, conducting an interview, taking minutes during a meeting, or videotaping an event and making a transcript of it
2. Analysis of the data and formulation of the first concepts by posing the question "What is happening here?" Researchers write down passages that seem to be important (relevant) on a concept card. This leads to reduction and combination of phrases. By means of reformulating, the researcher finally arrives at a definition of the concept that "fits" parts of the event. All concept cards together give as complete as possible a systematized description of the event. The result is a

collection of concept cards with titles, descriptions, and references to the raw data to which they belong.

3. Peer review: the concept cards are, together with the raw data to which they belong (transcript or tape), laid before independent reviewers

Specification

Specification involves:

1. Analysis of new data with the help of already-developed concepts that now act as sensitizing concepts and guide the process of searching. The new data lead to a refinement of the concepts and their description. Finally, the properties of the concept have to "fit" each example from the raw data that the researcher wants to describe.
2. Completion of the concept cards by interviews in the field
3. A search for a connection to existing theories by means of literature research; this step involves an investigation into possible connections between concept cards and theoretical concepts

This phase is complete when the researcher can code all new data within the set of concept cards and has developed the concepts' properties.

Reduction

Reduction is the development of the so-called core concept. The question that has to be answered is "What is the most important concept in all events?" Core concepts fulfill three criteria:

- They reflect the most important data.
- They show good cohesion with other concepts and take a central role.
- They reflect many raw data.

Integration

Integration is the development of a theory by fitting all concepts together, making hypotheses about relationships between concepts (for instance, causal, procedural), and testing the suggested relationships (hypotheses). The goal is to make an "integrative fit" around the core concept. The connection to existing theoretical models is researched, too. Strauss and Corbin (1990) have provided more developed definitions of the research tools that now predominate in this type of qualitative research, the most important of which are:

- **Concepts:** Labels placed on discrete happenings, events, and other instances of phenomena
- **Category:** A classification of concepts, discovered when concepts are compared against one another and appear to pertain to the same phenomenon. Concepts are grouped together under a higher, more abstract order.
- **Properties:** Attributes or characteristics pertaining to a category
- **Dimensions:** Location of properties along a continuum.
- **Axial Coding:** A set of procedures whereby data are put back together in new ways after open coding, by making connections between a category and its subcategories. This is done by using a coding paradigm involving conditions, context, action/interaction strategies, and consequences.
- **Core Category:** The central phenomenon around which all the other categories are integrated.
- **Selective Coding:** The process of selecting the core category, systematically relating it to other categories,

validating those relationships, and filling in categories that need further refinement and development

To illustrate, here is an example given by Strauss and Corbin (1990):

> While waiting for your dinner in a restaurant, you observe a woman in red standing in the kitchen. You are curious what she is doing there, just standing there in a busy kitchen. Your ask yourself, "What is she doing there?" First, you give a label to her behavior: *watching*. She also walks to somebody and tells him something. You label this *information passing*. Because she seems to notice everything, you label this *attentiveness*. She does not disrupt ongoing activities, which you call *nonintrusiveness*. Other labels that are linked to what she is looking for come to your mind: *efficiency* (of service), *quality* (of service), *timing* (of service). The woman sometimes gives *assistance,* and you have the impression that she is *experienced.*
>
> The way this labeling took place is conceptualizing, because you put concrete behavior (walking up to somebody and telling him something) into a concept *(information passing)*. Of course, sometimes there is only a slight difference between concrete labeling and conceptualizing *(watching)*. You also should be aware that conceptualizing can be interpretative.
>
> After labeling, concepts have to be grouped, like with like. Some of the concepts you introduced before— such as *watching* and *information passing*—can be put into the category *types of work to assess and maintain work flow*. Others—such as *attentiveness, nonintrusiveness,* and *experience*—are properties or conditions for this types of work. They fall into another category. Finally, you might decide that the job of the woman in red is *food orchestrator*. Call *food orchestrator* a category with two subcategories: *types of work to assess and maintain work flow* and *conditions for being a good food orchestrator*.

Dimension means that, for instance, *watching* can be often or less often, for a long period or a short one. *Frequency* and *duration* are then dimensions of *watching*.

In the previous example, we focused on the process. Now, here is an example of the final product. Strauss and Corbin (1990) give an example how the category *pain* has been specified, by *axial coding,* in terms of conditions, context, and strategies, which all are subcategories:

Causal Conditions: →→→→→→→→→→→ *Phenomenon:*
Broken leg   Pain

Properties of Broken Leg:
• Multiple fractures
• Compound break
• Sensation present
• Broken 2 hours earlier
• Occurred after fall in the woods

Dimensions of Pain:
• Intensity: high
• Duration: continuous
• Location: lower leg
• Trajectory: early
• Help obtained: after a long wait
• Potential for consequences: high

Pain Management Context:
Under conditions where pain is intense, continuous, located in lower leg, early in the trajectory, there is a long wait for help and the potential for consequences is high, then:

Strategies for Pain Management:
• Splint the leg
• Go for emergency help
• Keep the person warm

Intervening Conditions:
- Lack of training in first aid
- No blanket
- A long way to go for help

This model would be very helpful for music therapists because it has the structure "under conditions of ———, we treat like this . . ." In my own research method, I introduced the categories *disturbances* and *catalysts,* which come close to *intervening conditions.*

The core category is found when we ask ourselves "What is the essence of the story?" and select a category that ". . . is abstract enough to encompass all that has been described in the story" (Strauss and Corbin, 1990). Other categories become subsidiary categories and are related to the core category in terms of conditions, context, strategies, and consequences.

This example shows that grounded theory differs from other qualitative research paradigms in which causality is replaced by mutual simultaneous shapings (Lincoln and Guba, 1985). The model of "conditions-context-strategies-consequences" is a prefixed model; it is a theory how phenomena can be related. Thus, grounded theory is more positivistic in a paradigmatic sense.

GROUNDED THEORY IN
MUSIC THERAPY RESEARCH

An example of grounded theory research in music therapy is the work done by Amir (1992, 1993, 1996a). As a music therapist, she experienced moments in therapy that touched her strongly. When she tried to describe these moments, such words as *beauty, love, intuition, insight, peak experience, intimacy, spiritual, aha, transpersonal, transparent, aesthetic, creativity, flow of energy, contact, healing, transformation, change, growth, expansion, turning point, breakthrough, inspiration, catharsis, spontaneity, immediacy, liberation, openness,* and *oneness* came to her. She focused on these moments, asking herself how music therapy is experienced by the music therapist and the client.

The type of research question here shows that grounded theory was suited to answer this question. It was her aim to ". . . describe and understand the experience of music therapy— including the complexities of subjective realities and multilevel intrapersonal relationships and relationships between client(s), music, and therapist(s)—in an authentic manner" (Amir, 1996a). She needed a qualitative method because she was interested in the "subjective realities"; grounded theory was suitable because she was searching for concepts to describe meaningful moments. There were eight additional research questions (I have italicized the important words in each question):

About therapists:
1. *What* are the meaningful moments in the music therapy process as perceived by music therapists?
2. *How* do music therapists *describe* their experiences during these moments?
3. What is the *importance* of these moments to music therapists?

About clients:
4. *What* are the meaningful moments in the music therapy process as perceived by music therapy clients?
5. *How* do clients *describe* their experiences during these moments?
6. What is the *importance* of these moments to clients?
7. What are the *contributing* factors?
8. How do these moments *compare* when perceived and described by therapists versus clients?

The third/sixth and seventh questions show that Amir used grounded theory's axial coding. She was looking for connections between a category and its subcategories. A meaningful moment is a category; conditions (question 7) and consequences (question 3/6) are subcategories. As mentioned above, this coding paradigm in essence is in terms of causes and effects. For this reason, the criterion of "internal validity" is important.

Amir interviewed four music therapists and four clients. She used purposive sampling to choose participants who were most likely provide the best information for her study. Because this was a small group, intense contact between researcher and participant was possible. She used the ethnographic interview, developed by James Spradley, which she described as "a series of friendly conversations into which the researcher slowly introduces new elements to assist informants to respond as informants" (Amir, 1996a). She began interview with the question "When you think about your experience as a music therapist (or as a client in music therapy), what comes to your mind?" She used interview protocols, researcher's observer comments, process notes, and analytic memos as raw data. In analysis, her aim was to develop subcategories and discover core categories by means of reshaping and reorganizing. To ensure trustworthiness, Amir used intensive contacts with participants, member checking, peer debriefing, and negative case analysis.

To further explain, let us first go through the steps in the research process and then see how the results were obtained by following these steps.

Steps in the Research Process

The activities described here are from the researcher's perspective.

1. First step
   A. Record all interviews with an audiotape recorder and transcribe them.
   B. Add comments about your own feelings, thoughts, and impressions.
2. Second step
   A. Become familiar with the data by listening to the tapes and reading the transcripts.
   B. Make an initial categorization of each interview; for instance:
   - Category 1: background information
   - Category 2: examples of meaningful moments (first and fourth research questions: *what*)
   - Category 3: client's and therapist's feelings, images, reactions, explanations about the mean-

ing of the meaningful moments for them
(second and fifth research questions: *how*)

3. Third step
    A. Repeat step 2A.
    B. Extend step 2B; for instance, subdivide the
        third category and add new ones:
    • Category 3A: emotional reactions
    • Category 3B: physical reactions
    • Category 4: description of music
    • Category 5: description of context (see explana-
       tion of context above)

4. Fourth step
    A. Repeat step 2A.
    B. Find core categories and subcategories for each
        interview; for instance:
        Intrapersonal experiences:
    • Emotional (client/therapist)
    • Physical (client/therapist)
    • Spiritual (client/therapist)
        *Conditions that have allowed client/therapist to
        have these intrapersonal experiences:*
    • Self-perception (client/therapist)
    • Readiness/commitment (client)
    • Perception of music and music therapy
       (client/therapist)
    • Client–therapist relationship

5. Fifth step: Write a profile for each participant, con-
    taining background information of each person, a de-
    scription and analysis of each meaningful experience
    mentioned by the person, and a comparison of all the
    examples (cross-analysis of examples for each person)
    by means of three core categories:
    • Components and characteristics of all the ex-
       amples
    • Conditions that generated these experiences
       (seventh research question)
    • Contribution of these experiences to the par-
       ticipant's life (third and sixth research ques-
       tions); for instance:

Participant 1

	Example 1	Example 2	Example 3	Example 4
	→			
Characteristics→	→			
Conditions→	→			
Contributions→	→			

6. Sixth step
   A. Compare the profiles of the participants (cross-analysis of people).
   B. Compare the profiles by means of the three core categories of step 5. For instance:

	Participant 1	Participant 2	Participant 3	Participant 4
	→			
Characteristics→	→			
Conditions→	→			
Contributions→	→			

   C. Within *components and characteristics,* define *intrapersonal experiences* and *interpersonal experiences* as core categories and *components* and *characteristics* as subcategories. For instance:
   Client's intrapersonal experiences:
   • A sense of freedom
   • Sense of spirituality
   • Sense of intimacy
   • Insight
   • Sense of integration
   • Sense of being whole

7. Seventh step
   A. turn subcategories into meaningful moments:
   Subcategories:
   • A sense of freedom
   • A sense of spirituality
   • A sense of intimacy

- Insight
- A sense of integration
- A sense of being whole

Meaningful moments:

- Moments of freedom
- Moments of spirituality
- Moments of intimacy
- Moments of insight
- Moments of integration
- Moments of being whole

    B. Compare the meaningful moments of clients and music therapists.

8. Eighth step: Refine the meaningful moments by combining client's and therapist's moments that are alike.

9. Ninth step: Organize the findings into two sections:

- Profiles of four clients and four music therapists
- Second-level analysis that emerges from the previous step

In step 4, Amir handles *conditions* as a core category. In authentic grounded theory, however, it would be a subcategory of the core category *intrapersonal experience*. What becomes clear in step 4 is that categories in grounded theory say something about only the type of data. There are data about emotions and physical and spiritual reactions. Categories do not give us descriptions of these data; they just put data that of the same type into a box called *emotions* or *spiritual reactions*. In reading the interview transcripts, Amir found passages about emotions and physical and spiritual reactions.

In step 7, we might ask whether *a sense of freedom* is much more near to experience than *moment of freedom*. The reason why Amir turned *sense* into *moment* is not quite clear. Is it because she started her research with the intuition that there are meaningful moments?

In cross-analysis, we can use either an agreement or a cumulation model. In the former, only those characteristics that are alike in each example are selected; in the latter, distinct characteristics are cumulated. The former is intersubjective; the latter is multiple subjective. Amir used a cumulation model. For instance, in the core category *intrapersonal experiences,* she put together all meaningful moments experienced by participants, not meaningful moments experienced by all participants.

Results

General characteristics of meaningful moments:
- All moments were experienced on multiple levels (intra- and interpersonal, cognitive, physical, emotional, spiritual).
- All moments were difficult to describe.
- All moments happened spontaneously.

Meaningful moments in the music therapy process:
- Intrapersonal moments of:
  - Awareness/insight
  - Acceptance
  - Freedom
  - Wholeness/integration
  - Completion/accomplishment
  - Beauty/inspiration
  - Inner transformation
  - Spirituality
  - Intimacy with self
  - Ecstasy/joy
  - Anger, fear, pain
  - Surprise
  - Inner transformation
- Interpersonal moments of:
  - Physical closeness between client and therapist
  - Musical intimacy between client and therapist
  - Close contact between client and a significant person in his or her life

Factors that allowed these moments to come to birth:
- Environmental:
    - Music's stimulating the group to take risks, opening up areas, allowing them to experience new ways to relate, and giving delight and joy
    - Music therapy's stimulating the group to try new sounds and new ways of being, giving them a chance to be part of a bigger whole, and allowing anonymity.
- Intrapersonal factors of therapist:
    - Therapist's knowledge and experience
    - Therapist's listening to inner impulse, instinct, and intuition
    - Therapist's listening and exploration of the client's needs
    - Therapist's trust of his or her own knowledge, instinct, intuition, and impulse
    - Therapist's perception of "traveling together to unknown places" and supporting the client during the journey
    - Therapist's belief about personal growth
- Intrapersonal factors of client:
    - Client's attaching meaning to music
    - Client's feeling better about him- or herself
    - Client's readiness, inner motivation, and commitment to work
    - Client's courage to take risks
    - Client's perception of music therapy as a special place
    - Client's perception of the music therapist as knowledgeable and intuitive and of the relationship as intimate
    - Client's trust

Contribution to participant's life:
- To the client's life:
    - Improved self-esteem
    - Improved emotional and physical health
    - Improved interpersonal relationships

- To the therapist's life:
  - ◆ Improved therapeutic skill
  - ◆ Personal growth

Final Comments

If we adapt Strauss and Corbin's scheme, we see that several aspects were not specified:

- Causal conditions: not specified
- Phenomenon (client's problem): not specified
  - ◆ Properties: not specified
  - ◆ Dimensions: not specified
- Context: not specified
- Strategies: music therapy (not specified)
- Positive conditions:
  - ◆ Specific: music and music therapy group
  - ◆ Nonspecific: therapist's and client's intrapersonal factors
- Consequences:
  - ◆ During music therapy: intra- and interpersonal meaningful moments
  - ◆ In life: intrapersonal, interpersonal, and professional aspects in client and therapist

This type of research answers the question of what is experienced during music therapy, what factors were experienced as contributing, and which consequences were experienced. We see that the cause-and-effect pattern is within the participants' experience. Furthermore, we see that some aspects of the pattern are missing and should be addressed in future research: (1) the experienced characteristics of the clients' problems and (2) the experienced type of music therapy. There are a lot of nonspecific client and therapist conditional factors. Future research perhaps should focus more on the experienced importance of the specific factors of music therapy. Because the data all come from the participants' experiences, we do not know whether the clients' personal experiences correspond with observable changes in their psychological constitutions. This experience-focused type of research is of importance in the so-called client satisfaction assessment that today plays an important role in health care because the client is seen as a customer to be satisfied. We still should not forget that we can also assess clients' changes by tests or clinical opinion, keeping in mind that sometimes clients' self-reports and test outcomes do not correspond. I am saying not that the second method is more "objective" but that there are two perspectives of which we should be aware. An outcome such as meaningful moments and their consequences can reflect aspects of personal growth that are no guarantee that clients' disturbances have been "cured" to any extent. Because music therapists are "therapists," we must ask ourselves whether outcomes are relevant to clients' problems. In today's health-care climate, we are forced to formulate "indications" and answer the question of what intervention—how, when, and in which context—applied to which disturbance, for what reasons, can give which type of outcome. We therefore need to complete Strauss and Corbin's scheme.

I would like to point out that conditions and consequences sometimes are very close. For instance, "feeling better about yourself" is a condition, whereas "improved self-esteem" is a consequence. From this point of view, we can decide that music therapy must improve self-esteem, which then gives rise to meaningful moments that in turn influence self-esteem. From the vantage point of contributing factors, we also find that music therapy can be successful only when the client has "resources"—for instance, when music has some meaning for him or her. This again brings us to the question of indications. Above, we asked ourselves whether music therapy is relevant for the client's problem. Next, we should ask if music therapy will work with this particular client. It is beyond the scope of this book to answer these questions, but I bring them up because I want to illustrate that while Amir's research gives some interesting answers, it also gives rise to new, interesting research questions.

Chapter 6

FORMATION AND TRANSFORMATION
OF GESTALTS: MORPHOLOGY

GENERAL PRINCIPLES

The morphological method of music therapy is rooted in the morphological psychology of Salber (1965), who suggested that the psyche is generating and transforming forms all the time. The formation and transformation of gestalts is supposed to occur by means of six factors: appropriation *(Aneignung)*, metamorphosis *(Umbildung)*, influence *(Einwirkung)*, arrangement *(Anordnung)*, unfolding *(Ausbreitung)*, and equipment *(Ausrüstung)*. *Appropriation* means adopting something or being adopted by something, *metamorphosis* means changing or being changed, *influence* means causing something or being caused, *arrangement* means being limited by structure or finding a structure, *unfolding* refers to transcending experiences, and finally, *equipment* is the personal resources that make it possible to do something.

Küng (1995) gives an example of the effect of these factors—when someone buys a house. The house becomes part of his or her life (appropriation), he or she will rebuild some things (metamorphosis) and thereby influence it. When rebuilding, he or she must find a new or adjusted structure (arrangement). The way he or she influences the structure will depend on his or her skills, financial resources (equipment), and imagery (unfolding).

Music therapists influenced by morphological psychology are convinced that musical improvisation is the prototype of the formation of psychological gestalts because in music there is order, yet there is always transformation. Morphological music therapists claim that the way the psyche unfolds and transforms gestalts by these six factors can be heard in a musical improvisation. For them, there is no problem of "translation" from music to psychology because they believe that the same processes are expressed in both music and psychology. There is an analogous paradigm in morphology (Smeijsters, 1996a). In morphological music therapy, however, the analogy is described more explicitly and the analogous processes are categorized beforehand. This brings up an objection: although these factors certainly describe psychological processes, we could argue that they cannot describe the whole psyche satisfactorily. The same holds true for musical processes. These factors are part of a musical improvisation, but they cannot describe fully what is happening in musical improvisation. For instance, when a client imitates a music therapist's musical theme, he or she is appropriating it, but the term *appropriation* does not tell us whether it is melodic, rhythmic, or dynamic. Also, such processes as transference cannot be described satisfactorily by Salber's six factors. Morphological music therapists therefore need to also adopt concepts from other theories.

When we do qualitative research, the objection that we are taking only one perspective is not really a problem because we are not searching for "the" truth but giving our own perspective. This should be made very clear for any particular research project, however, because a model can very easily be interpreted as giving the whole truth. Also, a qualitative research strategy should be open enough to give a holistic impression. At this point in our discussion, it seems as if studying music therapy in view of these six factors gives only a limited—although legitimate—impression. We will discuss this in more detail later in this chapter.

The morphological qualitative research method is founded in the strong European nonpositivistic scientific tradition. For instance, Wilhelm Dilthey's view, as reported by Kühn (1975), that understanding *(Verstehen)* is needed when we are conducting research, an ever-changing phenomenon where there never can be a final definition and there can be only some kind of a deal between subject and object, comes very close to today's qualitative opinions. Although morphological researchers do not quote Lincoln and Guba (1985), their criticisms of quantitative research look very similar. Because there is a rich European tradition of qualitative research, one by which Lincoln and Guba were also influenced, European qualitative researchers have their own fundamental roots.

I will illustrate the criteria used by morphological researchers with the help of an article written by Tüpker (1990b, quoted also by Kühn, 1975). Although the discussion on criteria was part of Chapter 3 ("Reliability" and "Validity" in Qualitative Single-Case Research), I repeat her thoughts here because I think that her paper on this subject forms a bridge between the European qualitative research and the Anglo-Saxon naturalistic research traditions. Like Michele Forinash, David Gonzalez, Ken Aigen, and other "new paradigm" qualitative researchers, Tüpker starts by stating that we need a different research method because in art-therapy research, the traditional criteria for research are inadequate. As do Lincoln and Guba—who seem to be the source of new-paradigm research in music therapy—she focuses her critique on some of the criteria we discussed in Chapter 3: replicability, objectivity, and empiricism.

Replicability, the possibility of replicating at each point in time and place of the experiment, is impossible with people because no two people are alike, and even one person changes over time, according to Tüpker. This point of view is the same as the classic philosophical statement that you can never cross the same river twice. According to this idea, the "same" therapeutic intervention with different people at different moments will always have a different effect; it is impossible to use the "same" intervention because therapists, like their clients, differ and change over time. Here we see a close correspondence between morphological psychology, in which people are described as gestalt forms that are continuously being transformed, and principles of qualitative research.

Objectivity—guarding against subjective interpretations of the researcher and reactions of the research subject that result from the research setting (like social desirability)—is ensured in traditional research by the use of double-blind settings, standardized tests, and quantitative analyses. *Double blind* means that neither therapist nor subject know the real aim of the research. *Standardization* means observation using prefixed observation categories. As was discussed in Chapter 2, this makes it possible to compare the same characteristics in different people or to register changes in the same characteristics over time. Without standardization when observing the same person or comparing people, researchers risk comparing incomparable characteristics. Standardization makes it possible to use figures that can be computed. Objectivity exists in the purest sense when the outcome will always be the same, independent of the observer. Tüpker attacks the idea that subjectivity must be excluded. For her, this is undesirable and impossible. She believes that researchers must study experiences with an empathic attitude. This point of view is understandable in view of the therapeutic process: in therapy, a (music) therapist tries to understand the client through personal engagement. One "subject" tries to understand and communicate with another "subject."

If the therapeutic situation never can be "objective," then, Tüpker asks, does it make any sense that the research situation is "objective"? What can "objective" research tell us about a "subjective" situation? This point of view also leads directly to the conclusion that the (music) therapist—the one who is providing the treatment—is the best researcher, because the (music) therapist has the proper personal attitude. When the (music) therapist becomes the researcher, then "objectivity" is not only undesirable but also impossible.

Tüpker uses the word *empirical* as a concept for the experimental setting. I think, however, that the concept of *empiricism* should not become solely identified with *experiment* because naturalistic research, too, is empirical. Tüpker criticizes the experiment as a therapy research tool because in an experiment, independent variables are isolated and controlled, whereas in therapy, there is a "holistic process" without the possibility of changing specific (independent) variables' values, of stabilizing other variables' values, or of selecting (dependent) variables.

Like Lincoln and Guba, Tüpker replaces traditional research criteria with new ones. *Replicability* is transformed into *comprehensibility*, which gives another researcher the possibility of recapitulating the interpretation of the therapeutic process by investigating the detailed transcript. The second researcher verifies the chain of evidence. Consequently, the first researcher has to make a very detailed transcript. As with other research methods, this includes at least all raw data, the concepts and interpretations inferred from this data, and the reasons why (memos) they were inferred. Thus, the criterion of "comprehensibility" is satisfied. It is also clear that the traditional case study is *not* an adequate research instrument.

Objectivity is replaced by *controlled subjectivity*. The therapist/researcher has to develop insight into his or her own personal wishes, expectations, needs, and motives. Tüpker believes that self-experience, self-therapy, and supervision during the training of (music) therapists can ensure this. (In Chapter 3, we discussed the role of countertransference in research.) From her perspective—in which the (music) therapist is the researcher—this is an understandable conclusion. I wonder, though, whether it is sufficient to state that training as a researcher is concurrent with training as a therapist. *Controlled subjectivity* or *proved subjectivity* also means integrating the subjective reactions of the members of the research panel. Here, morphological researchers are traditional because they stress "intersubjectivity." Intersubjectivity as means of "objectivity" has been used in positivistic research, too.

Empirical (the experiment) is replaced by the *experience* of a trained observer who does not manipulate the naturalistic setting. To be able to observe, the music therapist/researcher needs to be trained. Just as one listening to a fugue has to learn to listen for several melodic lines, the music therapist/researcher has to learn which processes are developing synchronously during the therapy process. Here again, we might ask whether being able to listen to several musical voices is enough to allow the music therapist to become a researcher.

Finally, Tüpker mentions research criteria developed within morphological psychology (Salber, 1960) but similar to those developed in "new paradigm" qualitative research:

- **Mobility:** Being "open" to the phenomenon without formulating hypotheses or referring to existing models of therapy immediately
- **Wholeness:** Reconstructing the living, functional wholeness where details and totality supplement each other. Take care that details are not combined in a totality too quickly, with each single detail becoming subordinate to it. Take care also that you do not lose yourself in a jungle of details.
- **Meaning:** Being aware that the client's every musical action has some meaning and that you must try to understand this meaning
- **Essence:** Catching the essence. According to Salber, the essence lies not "behind" the phenomenon but "in" the phenomenon itself. This means that the musical

process is a psychic process and that the essence of the person expresses itself in the music. This idea, which I believe is very important in the development of a theory of music therapy, bridges the gap between the musical and the personal. As I proposed(Smeijsters, 1996a) in the theory of analogy and Pavlicevic (1989) proposed in her theory of dynamic forms, the musical process is a psychic process. We need to go beyond translating traditional musical language into traditional psychological language.

- **Integration:** Integrating the individual steps of treatment into a unity that makes sense.

What is striking here is that although they each may be from different theoretical backgrounds, many qualitative research methods often describe similar criteria and techniques. We can find, for instance, naturalistic, hermeneutic, and phenomenological aspects. Thus, qualitative research methods do not depend entirely on the psychological or therapeutic school to which their particular proponents belongs but share common ground. In Chapter 3, I explained my own ideas about research criteria; therefore, I will not repeat them here.

MORPHOLOGICAL RESEARCH
IN MUSIC THERAPY

As you may conclude from the section above, the scientific criteria of morphological research very closely resemble the naturalistic criteria developed by Lincoln and Guba (1985), among others. Now let us look at an example of morphological research (Tüpker, 1983). At the start of her description of this particular study, Tüpker again emphasizes the importance of subjectivity in research. She concludes that music is a subjective phenomenon and thus must be described in a manner appropriate for subjectivity. To me, it seems that positivistic science is identified too often with an outdated behavioral methodology. Of course, it is true that in behaviorism, "introspection" was considered suspect because positivistic science searches for "the" truth and introspection cannot guarantee that events really unfolded the way

any one researcher describes them. Phenomenological researchers, however, look not for truth but for experience. One might say
that in phenomenology, experience as such is "true." This description, however, is not black and white, because in positivistic
methodology, it is possible to include subjectivity. "Self-reports,"
even if they are standardized, include subjectivity, and every
assessment tool can include questions about subjective experiences. Standardization and quantification themselves are not
antithetical to subjectivity. What has been excluded in positivistic
methodology is the uniqueness of the person under study and the
subjectivity of the researcher.

Tüpker states that music is a subjective phenomenon,
which means that when listening to music, people experience
feelings, thoughts, images, and so on. As we already know, it is
supposed in morphological thinking that musical processes *are*
psychological processes, that art expression can explain the
psyche, and that it is possible to "reconstruct" the psyche of the
client from an improvisation. Central to the reconstruction
method is the description and exchange of subjective experiences
by a panel of four to six coresearchers. The first morphological
research group consisted of Tüpker, Grootaers, Weber, and
Weymann; Kühn (1995) writes that members of this panel can be
colleagues, musicians, or friends who are competent listeners and
are able to express their feelings. There are several more qualitative strategies that use "resonating panels" (for instance, see
Langenberg et al., 1992, 1993, 1996). The "countertransference"
that is evoked by this method is discussed later in this chapter.
This qualitative method differs with other methods, in which the
client's verbal descriptions are included from the start.

There are four steps in morphological methodology,
described below (see also Kühn, 1995).

First Step: Wholeness

Researchers react to an improvisation as a whole, giving
their complete impressions, and write down their subjective
experiences (images, stories, memories, impressions). As in other
forms of qualitative research, the researchers become the research

instrument. In a case involving a 25-year-old client, researchers reacted to an audio recording of the first improvisation as follows:

- "Starving"
- "To keep for your own, to sit on the lavatory for hours"
- "Everything in the music is cut off."
- "Power because of weakness"
- "After a short period, everything has been said, but it could continue endlessly."
- "The only thing to do is leave."
- "I want to switch off the tape."
- "Mirroring and imitating: who is who?"
- "Nothing comes into being; it is rotating."

These descriptions are founded in phenomenology because they are prescientific impressions. Preselected codes from existing theories are excluded.

By means of exchange and comparison among members of the research group, the researchers create a summary and find a title or metaphor that characterizes their impressions. Here, we can clearly see the resemblance to grounded theory. In this example, the word *stowage* was used. Because the title should be grounded in the data, every subjective impression has to be linked to it. For instance: *stowage* can be linked to *keep for your own.* It can also be linked to *deficit,* which in turn can be linked to starving and being cut off. Some of the impressions were interpreted as "effects," as a result of trying to escape the pressure—for instance, "leav[ing]" and "switch[ing] off the tape." Other impressions were interpreted as the means by which the stowage becomes possible: "power because of weakness," "mirroring and imitating," and "rotating."

We can see that from the first concept—"stowage"—the research group generated a theoretical framework with which impressions could be connected. "Stowage" is the core theme from which categories, such as "effects" and "means," emerged. This "theory" can be submitted to the criteria of "construct validity," "objectivity," and "internal validity": is "stowage" the most credible concept to be used here? Is the grounding in the data free from biased interpretations? Is it easily confirmed? Are the interconnections among "stowage," "deficit," and the proposed effects and means credible?

Second Step: Inside Regulation

In exploring how holistic impressions arise through processes in the musical microstructure, researchers look into the details. The research group operates with two criteria: (1) the details should correspond to the whole and (2) the whole should be confirmed by the details. To illustrate the holistic impressions of the first research step, I have chosen a description of an excerpt of the musical improvisation:

- The client does not play.
- The therapist plays a chord, then waits.
- There is a pause.
- The therapist plays another chord.
- There is a pause.
- The therapist plays a melodic question.
- There is a pause.
- The client starts playing very softly.
- The therapist plays with the client.
- The client stops.

When we choose a detail, it is important that it be somehow representative to exclude selection bias. Thus, selection must be "reliable": will the same detail be chosen a second time or by a second researcher as being an important detail? How does the group discussion contribute to this selection of details? One negative aspect of group discussions might be that the person with the most influence forces (persuades) others to comply. Another is that in groups, there are never truly independent answers. Nevertheless, using a group discussion rather than the analysis of a single researcher makes the study stronger.

The detail also needs to be "valid": does this detail represent holistic impressions? The interpretation of the research group in the above sample case was as follows: (1) "The client does not want to play synchronously"; (2) "There is an imbalance between therapist and client." The first point was interpreted as the client's taking care of distance. The second point was linked to the first research step: although the therapist tried to abolish the imbalance by gradually reducing his musical offerings, the client in fact—by hesitating (being weak)—influenced how and when the therapist played music, which is reflected in the panel member's description of "power because of weakness." We could argue that it is not clear if the client experienced this "power"; the experiences of the research group gave rise to the concept of power. They concluded that "stowage" occurred because the client did not answer the therapist's musical invitations and pauses occurred.

Later on in the improvisation, the client imitated the music therapist's playing. When the therapist, reacting to this, imitated the client's imitating, then the client initiated new sounds. The researchers linked this passage to the holistic impression "Who's who?" These behaviors then were interpreted as parts of a "method of life" that the researchers supposed could be found in the client's daily life.

Before we proceed to the next research step, I must make two objections. First, the researchers who wrote down the holistic impressions are the same ones who interpreted the details. Because they had already determined several meanings of their impressions in the first research step, perhaps in step 2 they interpreted the details in a way that they would correspond with the already existing holistic impressions. Perhaps this criticism resembles positivistic thinking, but in qualitative research, two distinct groups of researchers can be used to maximize the potential disagreement. One group of researchers can give holistic impressions and another—unaware of these impressions—can select and interpret details. Second, when the group was making hypotheses, they did not consider other possibilities, or at least they did not report them. Sometimes it looks as if all pieces fit together perfectly, whereas in qualitative research, they may not always do so, and thus hypotheses must be adjusted all the time. So that we—and others later—can check the chain of evidence, we must write down the uncertainties and the fragments that do not fit and report the struggle for meaning. Kühn (1995) refers to this as a multiple determination and cautions researchers to always be aware of contradictions. These contradictions should be written down in the research report, too, to ensure controlled subjectivity.

Third Step: Transformation

The third research step builds on what the researchers in the sample case referred to in step 2 as a "life method." At this point, the researchers must explore whether the musical improvisation that they analyzed represents the whole or only one part of the client. This research step resembles "specification" in grounded theory, or negative case analysis, when researchers look to other data—which can include other improvisations, communications, behaviors inside or outside music therapy, and biographical information—to corroborate, change, complete, or contradict their findings.

In this step, other possibilities are considered, but the interpretation of the first improvisation still will be taken for granted while the other data are used to see how the first improvisation fits into the whole personal picture. The researchers describe how the body language of the client corresponded to the musical play: the client walked very slowly, did not talk a lot, and did not initiate talking. There seemed to be an analogy between musical and nonmusical behavior. In the second improvisation, however, when an accelerando came up, the client took over leadership, raised the tempo, and stayed with it. For the researchers, it seemed to be a sound "trip." The client did not stop and tried to lengthen the musical climax infinitely. The client himself illustrated the music with the metaphor of "a picture cast in tin," representing "snow." The researchers associated this with the likelihood that once, the client must have had an inner fire that was then put out, leaving rigidity without transformation.

Fourth Step: Reconstruction

The last step of research, as in grounded theory, is to reconstruct a "local theory" about the client as a result of the first three steps. This is meant to lead to a higher level of consciousness. To understand the client's individual processes, researchers use the more general theory of morphological psychology, in which formation and transformation are the fundamental concepts used in explaining psychological phenomena. As described earlier in this chapter, it is supposed in morphology that six gestalt factors organize the formation and transformation of psychological phenomena: appropriation, metamorphosis, influence, arrangement, unfolding, and equipment.

In the particular research example we are discussing, the researchers asked themselves (1) how the two improvisations could be connected and (2) what was not allowed a chance to develop in either session. They concluded that in both improvisations, there was no metamorphosis. In the first one, the client had chosen restriction to exclude metamorphosis. The reason for this, they suggested, was that the client did not develop his music because he did not want it to be influenced by the music therapist, and formation would have taken place, which would have curtailed possibilities. The client would have then lost his omnipotence. To me, it seems as if in this interpretation several conceptual chains are made that should be open to discussion. It is not clear if the client really experienced this fear of losing omnipotence.

In the researchers' interpretation, the client needed the second improvisation as compensation, so that he could satisfy the need that had been inhibited in the first one. From another perspective, I would say the client curtailed himself in the first improvisation so as not to be curtailed. The theory of pragmatic paradoxes would have made this paradox understandable.

The researchers used morphological psychology to conceptualize the findings, and it looks as if their theory fits the data very well. As you can see at the end of step 3, however, the factors of morphological psychology were already present in the data. Consequently, it is not surprising that the researchers could use the factors of morphological psychology in step 4. The research bias that researchers put into the data what they want to get out of it can easily be resolved by using independent qualitative researchers, including more theoretical frameworks, and conceiving the morphological interpretation as one single perspective.

There are several similarities to grounded theory in morphological research methods. Within the context of the above four research steps, it is very clear what researchers are looking for, but it is less clear what methods they use in proceeding through these steps.

Chapter 7

WRITING STORIES

INTRODUCTION

Kenny (1996a) describes her work with Debbie, who became a quadriplegic because of an accident and had a severely disfigured face, drooled incessantly, and was nourished by a nasogastric tube. The nursing staff had declared her case hopeless, but Kenny felt attracted to her and started to work with her in music therapy. When working with Debbie, Kenny experienced beauty, but her attempts to describe progress in quantifiable language produced nothing meaningful. She tried to complete chart information and realized that she was standardizing her client, that individuality was lost. As we have discussed in previous chapters, standardization is a means to describe things within the same framework. It makes it easy for us to compare states in the same person over time and between people. Of course, when we observe different people and events within the same framework, we get only what can fit the framework, losing what falls through. If we want to make comparisons, frameworks can be useful. If we do not, but wish instead—like Kenny—to describe experience directly, frameworks are of little help. They are indirect because they were constructed before the experience itself. As with phenomenology, we must put aside preconstructions to describe experience directly.

It is striking that in quantitative research, researchers always feel compelled to make comparisons by using standardization, as if this tells us more about human beings. The truth is that it tells us less, that it makes all things equal. So that we can understand more about qualitative research, let us see which philosophical and methodological influences shaped Kenny's professional development.

PHILOSOPHICAL AND
METHODOLOGICAL BACKGROUND

In her work *The Field of Play* (1989), Kenny bases her research method on the idea that ". . . we must be doing, or at least vividly remembering, music therapy experience while designing philosophy and theory". She wants to be in touch with the "direct experience," to be in the "immediacy of experience," using "tacit knowing" as resource. She is looking for a research method that is both artistic and scientific, searching for objective truth and subjective meaning at the same time. Kenny connects *meaning* to "creating images that people find meaningful," which is a matter of art. The first idea that comes to my mind when reading this is that if art gives meaning by images, then perhaps we should claim that the "artistic method" reveals more than does scientific research.

We should ask ourselves why we need scientific research methods when art can give us meaning, when art—as Kenny points out—can make us aware of things because of the sensations artistic images give us. Why do we have to translate this direct consciousness into scientific concepts, removed from immediate experience, and exchange our tacit knowledge for more explicit knowledge? This book is not the appropriate arena in which to answer this complex question—this idea has been explored elsewhere (Smeijsters, in preparation)—but I want to add a caveat. Kenny's line of reasoning, which takes us from direct sensory experience to consciousness, is built on the proposition that consciousness is being conscious of our senses (visual, auditory, tactile, and so on). This is a sensualistic image of humankind.

Although art alone could be a sufficient conduit for meaning, Kenny does not reject science as such but tries to find an artistic philosophy of science, which like art, creates images. In phenomenology, she finds what she is looking for, because phenomenology tries to create images of direct experiences of phenomena. She also uses concepts from hermeneutics, heuristic

inquiry, and systems and field theories. With the help of hermeneutics, direct experiences (figures) are interpreted with the
whole background of our being in the world. Heuristic inquiry, as
described in Chapter 4, makes use of self-experience. Like gestalt
psychology did for perception, systems theory focuses on the
psychosocial aspects of the relationships between parts. Kenny
quotes Mircea Eliade, who believes there is a primordial order
that gives meaning to a relational structure. As in phenomenology, preknowledge in systems theory is put aside when describing
this primordial order, which as Jose Argüelles proposed, can be
done only on an intuitive level by suspending civilized, logical,
and technical knowing. In field theory, a system is described as an
interplay of forces in a context in which boundaries do not exist
but a maximum interdependence does.

The search for essential elements of music therapy is
supported by a process of dialoguing, comparing, and contrasting
within a panel of music therapists and another of other professionals (dance/movement therapist, psychiatrist, neuropsycholo-
gist, existential phenomenologist, musicologist, composer, acu-
puncturist). The first panel develops the concepts and definitions.
Members of the second panel are asked by a questionnaire
whether they experienced these concepts and definitions when
looking at and listening to a videotape of clinical improvisation.

Kenny's research perspective can be summarized as being
a search for meaning among interrelated forces by means of
immediate (self-)experiences, excluding presuppositions, before a
background of wholeness. One of the research tools she uses is
free fantasy variation. In eidetic reduction (imaginative variation), as
in phenomenology (described in Chapter 4), characteristics of the
phenomenon are exchanged, subtracted, or added to see if the essence
changes. Kenny describes *free fantasy variation,* as Edmund Husserl
does, as an intuitive process in which ". . . various possibilities of what
may be examples, pictures, or images of the phenomenon [are exam-
ined] in order to determine what are its essential elements."

The two-panel element is a very strong point in this
research design. To use it, music therapists must be sure to
develop their own descriptive language that is easily understood
by other professionals.

In another paper (1996b), Kenny calls free fantasy variation an "intramember check," working with a panel within the
music therapy field an "intermember check," and working with

professionals from other fields an "extramember check." This third member checking she sees as a tool to assess "validity." Although she uses the term *member checking* in a slightly different manner here, her three categories can add to our understanding of the feedback process. (In naturalistic research, *member checking* means checking our interpretations with the people we are studying [the music therapist and/or the client], and *peer debriefing* means working with a support group [Lincoln and Guba, 1985; Ely et al., 1995].) The intramember check is part of reflective phenomenology, but unlike some other reflective phenomenologists, Kenny uses confirmation by others. Inter- and extramember checking in fact are peer debriefings.

A final point about this research method is the value of stories. In *The Field of Play* (1989), Kenny writes:

> Stories describe life. They gather tradition. They lay a groundwork and reflect the implied patterns of experience. They inspire the imagination. They communicate "immediacy," the rhythm, tone, and texture of our life on Earth. In the ancient traditions, the terms *story* and *song* were interchangeable. Song carries spirit.

Telling a story is making use of imaginative narrating while staying close to experience. There is a link between free fantasy variation and storytelling because the music therapist/researcher can tell many stories about the same experience that lead him or her to "essential elements." The story, according to Kenny, is "fiction." Stories resulting from free fantasy variation lead to intrasubjective "comparative fiction," which, as has pointed out before, can be supplemented by inter- and intracomparative fiction. When I read about "essential elements," I suspect that the phenomenological search for these elements somehow makes use of quantitative thinking within a conventional paradigm. Because something appears many times, because it is replicated in many descriptions, it is defined as essential. There seems to be some final "truth" when something is stripped of all unnecessary things. This is the way many of us are used to handling these things; it is the way I used to handle member checking and peer debriefing. Another perspective would be to look at the variations and to describe how things can vary. Then we are searching not for "essentials" but for "variations." Telling stories about music therapy can be like describing improvisations: we can listen for what is the same or for what changes. There is no conservation without variation and vice versa, but in research, looking at conservation seems to be more important, whereas variations are as essential as recurring themes.

Kenny uses such words as *dynamic* and *ambiguity,* and she believes it is a paradox that she is using a method to find definitions grounded in essentials despite being leery of definitions because they seem not to leave "room for life" (Kenny, 1996a). She quotes Taylor and Bogdan (1984), who give several important and influential characteristics of qualitative research:

- Inductive
- Holistic (not reduced to variables)
- Nonintrusive
- Understanding from the participant's frame of reference
- Viewing things as if they were happening for the first time (phenomenological)
- Holding all perspectives as valuable
- Amenable to researching humanistic concepts (beauty, pain, love, and so on)
- Staying close to the empirical world (without operationalizations)
- Holding all settings and people as worth studying
- Viewing qualitative research as a craft

For Kenny, one of the most important characteristics is the use of descriptive data: people's own written or spoken words and observable behavior. She further argues, in line with Taylor and Bogdan's thinking, that many researchers choose quantitative methods because variables, operational definitions, and rating scales offer a less complex reality. She goes so far as to quote Taylor and Bogdan, saying that this method is an ". . . incorrect course with a maximum of precision." She clearly rejects quantitative research, but she does not quote Lincoln and Guba; therefore, we cannot deduce that her stance on the objectivity and subjectivity of naturalistic inquirers is as radical. She favors a research method that is both objective and subjective at the same time. This means that she favors not quantitative research but objectivity from the phenomenologist's point of view: a search for essentials by means of "validation." We could say she takes a middle position in the battle over paradigms.

What strikes me particularly is that Kenny, besides being rooted in phenomenology and the Native American culture, makes use of critical social theory. She quotes Theodor Adorno, an important representative of the Frankfurt school, and refers to Herbert Marcuse, who began as a member of the Frankfurt school and exerted a major influence in the 1960s. By doing so, Kenny gives her discussion of qualitative research a background unique in music therapy theory. Let us take a short trip into critical theory. What Horkheimer and Adorno, in the *Dialektik der Aufklärung* (1981), make clear to us is that, since the eighteenth century, there has been a tendency to manipulate nature and human beings: language and science have become the tools by which we control these "things." In science, numbers are used to make incomparable phenomena comparable. Thus, everything has become comparable, general, replicable, formed along standards. Individuals have lost their uniqueness because they have become examples of the general. The process of understanding has been reduced to mechanical procedures that give us numbers. As Horkheimer and Adorno say (1981), "It has become impossible to hear new sounds with your own ears, to see new things with your own eyes, and to understand things with your own mind." The concept of *truth* has been identified with the scientific method. Understanding has been formalized and has become a fetish. Imagination and spontaneity have withered. Nothing changes; things are produced mechanically and reproduced. Horkheimer and Adorno's critique of the scientific method comes close to Abraham Maslow's description of science as a machine, run by noncreative people, that produces noncreative products.

Kenny quotes Horkheimer and Adorno: ". . . Method must constantly do violence to unfamiliar things, though it exists only so that they may be known. It must model itself after the other." Then she continues: "In other words, there is an integrity between the experience and the method. Yet in this case, knowledge, as method, creates sorrow because it takes us away from, even does violence to, experience" (Kenny 1996a). The message is clear: scientific method makes us deaf, it is removed from life, it shrinks personal understanding, and it tries to exclude mistakes by excluding personal involvement. This exclusion is a trend in our society. Everything is seen as needing to be under control because it is part of complex constellations that cannot work without a huge amount of control. Human beings are assimilated into schemes and structures. Horkheimer and Adorno's critique of modern Western society and Kenny's experiences of Native American culture meet at this point. From these views, we can understand why qualitative researchers try to reestablish researchers themselves as research instruments. It really is strange that in conventional science, only methods and (nonhuman) measuring instruments are seen as reliable, as if human beings are unable to understand life.

In Horkheimer and Adorno's opinions, science is used as a means to control. The individual's uniqueness is lost with a scientific method that tries to make all things comparable, ignores anything nonstandardized, and guarantees replication of the same events and data by standardization. These are very fundamental questions: Do we need to control? Do we need to make phenomena comparable? Do we need to replicate and predict? A science that chooses to define "laws" of prediction, which make it possible to control people, is based on the paradigmatic value that humans can be replicated and predicted, but a science that describes the unique and unpredictable is based on the value that people need support to change in a personal, unpredictable way. What I am saying is that the choice itself is paradigmatic; it cannot be "proven." Both options are viable, and the choice you make comes from your own life philosophy.

In Chapter 3, I stated that the choice between quantitative and qualitative research is a matter of research topic. If you as a music therapist are interested in the unique personal development of people in a specific context, then you need a research paradigm in line with this. If you are looking for "general laws of human behavior," however, then you need a different research paradigm. I think we should not forget that we need "methods" to cope with life. Every person has a "life method," a way to look at and handle things. The paradox is that what can be of help in coping with life can be also a constraint on experiencing life. When a method does not change and adapt itself to new circumstances, when it becomes a schematic for controlling life, then we lose life, we lose ourselves, and our fellow human beings. There always will be methods because people, and thus researchers, are unable to live without them, but we also need to have the courage to change our methods, to be open, to take risks, to make mistakes, to go into an experience without being pressed into a methodological armor.

Some of my colleagues claim that we as therapists should choose only the value of uniqueness. To be honest, sometimes I doubt whether it is really a matter of choice, because I think that what really counts in life, in therapy, and in research is the person as a unique human being. I hesitate to completely abandon positivistic science conducted in service of critical theory, however, because I believe critical theory itself reduces positivistic theory to a caricature. Even in therapy research, the uniqueness and variability of human beings are not always the most important aspects. Sometimes we need general information to help us be better prepared to benefit clients. Let me say it differently: the unique personality often develops within a general pattern of human existence.

As we have seen, Kenny uses definitions, but she wants to embed ambiguity. This ambiguity, in terms of dialectic theory, plays an important role in critical theory. When we are describing phenomena, are we just describing what is or do we leave space for what can be? This again shows the difference between replication and variation: the quantitative researcher looks for replication, while the qualitative researcher searches for variation. Here Kenny appears to side with qualitative researchers, saying that method violates unfamiliar things.

I have one final personal comment. Perhaps my walk to and from the quantitative and qualitative paradigms is not clear-cut. It is a result of my dialogue with qualitative researchers since the First Symposium for Qualitative Reserach (in Düsseldorf, Germany, 1994). My dialogue with Carolyn Kenny especially reminded me of my early explorations of the writings of Adorno and Marcuse, about which I wrote theses. My position in the research discussion seems to be on an island, building bridges to different continents. I remember David Aldridge, who in his epilogue in Düsseldorf talked about building bridges, so it seems that I am not completely isolated. Perhaps not sailing to one of the continents is a mistake, but I do not want to "solve" this dilemma now. If, as Ken Bruscia reminds us, we need to study our personal authenticity, then I invite you to my island to share my unsolved dilemma. I hope that you will not be disturbed by this trip but will experience the excitement of the dialogue.

THE FIELD OF PLAY

As we discussed above, a system in field theory is described as an interplay of forces in a context in which there are not boundaries but maximum interdependence. Field theories describe forces, conditions, and qualities. In her *Field of Play* (1989), Kenny describes a theory of music therapy with the help of field theory. This theory was a result of a research process in which, by means of free fantasy variation and peer debriefings, a new language was developed that describes essential elements of music therapy, its concepts, and their interrelationships. Kenny defines three primary and four secondary fields and the conditions establishing each field. Where the field theorist Kurt Lewin introduced a personal life space, Kenny introduces a musical space. The following is a summary of her findings.

Primary Fields

The primary fields include:

- **The Aesthetic:** A field of beauty that is the human person and all nonverbal cues that are perceived intuitively. There is the aesthetic of the client and that of the music therapist.
- **The Musical Space:** An intimate and private field—a contained space—created between the therapist and client, similar to the space created between mother and child in early childhood
- **The Field of Play:** A space of experimentation, modeling, and imitation in sound forms that express, represent, and communicate significant feelings, thoughts, attitudes, values, behavioral orientations, and issues of growth and change

Secondary Fields

Secondary fields include:

- **Ritual:** Constants and repetitions that are a sacred ground base, sounds and behaviors that are repeated over the course of the session
- **A Particular State of Consciousness:** A state of deep concentration and focused attention that makes a person receptive to new experiences, forms, and sounds
- **Power:** The cumulative energy that draws a person into new possibilities, a dialogue between inner strength and significant external resources
- **Creative Process:** The interplay of forms, gestures, and relationships that as a whole constitute the context for a movement toward wholeness, informed by love, the intelligence of the heart, and knowledge of the self-organizing system

Discussion

The "driving force" in this theory is the natural creative self-organization of the client that, in safe circumstances and with appropriate resources, leads to reorganization. Each field has conditions that establish the field. A condition is anything that determines a field; for instance, "love" and "existential attitude" in the field of the aesthetic, "commitment" and "containment" in the musical space, "a value for play and modeling" and "openness" in the field of play, and so on.

I have several comments. By her use of "concepts," Kenny wants to give us tools that can be part of a new language to describe music therapy. This language has been developed by writing many stories about one session with a client (free fantasy variation), then asking music therapists how they would describe the musical improvisation, and finally asking other professionals, on questionnaires, if they could ". . . see or hear or sense or perceive in any way an aesthetic, a musical space, a field of play, ritual, a particular state of consciousness, power, or creative process as described." These professionals gave feedback by which the definitions of the fields were refined. Kenny points out that the "eidos" is not universal and that it reflects her personal experience with clients. Thus, a concept like *the aesthetic* is a result of the fact that Kenny, when working with her clients, experienced "beauty" and then was interested in whether other music therapists have the same experience.

She is "validating" her personal perspective on music therapy, a perspective she developed in her experience as a music therapist. She offers a scheme for the peer debriefings that makes "open coding" impossible. I believe that many conceptual schemes can be "validated" this way, because music therapy can give rise to many types of descriptions and conceptualizations. Because the music therapists in the first panel were members of the Phoenecia group, I suggest that these colleagues' perspectives were already close to Kenny's. We might ask, then, which conceptual scheme would have been developed if another music therapist had done the free fantasy variation and if another group of colleagues had been used. Using Kenny's methods, it seems as if something personal (not universal) is being studied in order to make it impersonal (universal). This is different from combining your personal perspective with the personal perspectives of others and thus creating multiple perspectives.

We must also discuss further the different types of essentials found in her method: the essentials within the many stories of one person and the essentials within the stories of different people. We can ask ourselves if the words used in Kenny's personal perspective "fit" the multiple experiences of music therapists working with different client groups. Does Kenny's conceptual scheme finally tell each music therapist what he or she is doing? I do not think so. To me, this conceptual scheme looks too general. Its strength is that it can be used for almost every therapy, but in a dialectical way, this strength also turns out to be its weakness. The theory does not tell us a lot about what a music therapist is doing when working with a specific client group.

Some of the words she uses are confusing. For instance, the word *aesthetic* is unclear because it is so connotatively determined. What is more, by saying that the human being is an "aesthetic," she proposes a link between human beings and an aesthetic therapy, like music therapy, which is metaphoric but can give us few arguments for why music therapy is indicated.

The word *love,* in the context of therapy, can be confusing, too. These words are so ordinary that it looks as if the theory of music therapy is equal to human life phenomena. The reader is being forced to translate these words into the more specific meanings Kenny implies. From a conventional scientific perspective, this seems inadequate, but perhaps we should again change our perspective. Although these words, in my opinion, do not tell us a lot about music therapy, they give us some essentials about human relationships, which are part of music therapy. A person should be able to experience another person, with all of his or her characteristics, just the way he or she is, as a work of art. Of course, we can use such terms as *respect* and *unconditional positive regard,* introduced by Carl Rogers, or *I and thou,* by Martin Buber, but *the aesthetic* gives us the sense of another human being, and *love* gives us the sense of intimacy with another human being.

Chapter 8

RESONATING WITH THE
MUSIC THERAPY PROCESS

INTRODUCTION

In several research methods described in the previous chapters, researchers' experiences are an important tool. When they use personal thoughts, images, stories, and feelings, qualitative researchers act like music therapists, who depend on their own experiences to understand the client, the relationship, and the music. Qualitative researchers' often-used statement that "the researcher is the instrument" refers to the researcher's serving as the "measuring instrument." The important role of these personal experiences in qualitative research has led several music therapists who are also researchers to conclude that the music therapist him- or herself should serve as the researcher. Researchers who do not share this point of view combine the subjective experiences of the music therapist with the experiences of the client and/or the experiences of panel members. Being your own researcher has the advantage that your data come from the therapist who is closest to the process of therapy, but there is the disadvantage of not having multiple perspectives from different people. We will discuss whether therapists should serve as their own researcher in Chapter 9.

In the following chapters, experience is important and the methods described and analyzed have characteristics of phenomenology, grounded theory, and morphology. In this chapter, however, we focus on the aspect of experience in a research method that uses a panel that is not a prototype of phenomenology, grounded theory, or morphology.

THE RESONATOR FUNCTION

The research method of Langenberg et al. (1992, 1993, 1996) uses a panel and is descriptive and interpretative (Tesch, 1992). It resembles morphological research in that it is used to analyze a single improvisation, but it differs in that the panel is formed by the music therapist, the client, observers, and musicians. The music therapist can be the researcher, but it is possible, too, for the researcher to be one of the observers. Triangulation of investigators is used, the participant's subjectivity is sought, and countertransference becomes a research tool.

Langenberg et al. conceptualized the subjective impressions of the members of the panel as serving a "resonator function," a concept that, because of its auditory impact, is perhaps more appropriate than concepts with a visual impact, such as "mirroring" or "reflecting." Another advantage of this concept is that it emphasizes the fact that the countertransference occurs through a musical medium. Here, the idea that the researcher is the instrument is used as a metaphor: the researcher (and each member of the panel) is like a musical instrument that resonates when another instrument is sounding. This is a strong metaphor, but we should keep in mind that it is not an analogy (Smeijsters, 1996a). The resonating of a musical instrument in essence is *not* the same as the resonating of a human being, the first being a physical process and the second, a psychological process. In the early history of music therapy, this difference was often ignored.

The members of the panel "resonate." The improvisation they listen to is "resounded" in their psyche, and they try to translate this verbally. Contrary to those music therapy researchers who stress that the music therapist should be the researcher, Langenberg et al. have independent people, who take no part in the improvisation and are not informed about it, give their impressions. This resembles the double-blind rule of positivistic research. As we will see, intersubjectivity, not multiple perspectives, is sought in this method. It is interesting to see that a qualitative research method that is really qualitative because a naturalistic situation is described subjectively also preserves methodological aspects that are not completely contrary to positivistic rules. Looking for recurrences in the subjective descriptions seems to be a way to control for the countertransferences that are part of the personal biography and not grounded in the improvisation. We can best understand this research method through a description of the steps involved.

Step 1: Producing Data

The members of the panel are asked to describe freely their impressions when listening to the improvisation, to freely give their feelings, thoughts, images, and stories.

Step 2: Categorizing Qualities

As with Dorit Amir's method of grounded theory, each individual description is categorized first and then all descriptions made by panel members are cross-analyzed. Two categories, called qualities, are used to categorize the individual descriptions:

1. Content: images, scenes, fantasies, histories
2. Feelings:
   A. Feelings indicated in the music, reflections, and evaluations
   B. Feelings experienced by the listener: affects, emotions, moods, evaluations, and reflections not describing the music but belonging to the personal reaction to this music

The further division of category 2 into subcategory 2A and subcategory 2B has been made by several receptive music therapists, too: "What do you think is expressed by this music?" versus "What do you experience yourself?" Although it is possible to make a distinction between the subcategories, both refer to the subjectivity of the listener. For example, "Descriptions that give the experience a place in the evaluative and normative perspective of the listener" belong to subcategory 2A. "Values and reflections that belong not to the music but to the personal reactions to music" belong to subcategory 2B. In both cases, the evaluations are grounded in the personal evaluative and normative perspective. The same holds true for the sentences "This music is aggressive" and "This music makes me aggressive." When I describe the feelings that are expressed in music, I project meaning from my own experience. This does not mean that I am experiencing this feeling now, and therefore a distinction can be made. It should be mentioned, however, that save for conventional interpretations, category 2A is as subjective as category 2B.

While Amir, as a grounded theorist, makes a cross-analysis of each interview to refine the categories, Langenberg et al. define the categories beforehand. Although Langenberg et al. claim this to be an inductive way of working, it is not. When we look closer at Amir's work, we see that after refining the categories, she comes up with such categories as "components," "conditions," and "contributions." Strauss and Corbin (1990) use what they call a "paradigm" ("conditions, context, strategies, consequences") when specifying a category or related categories. This brings us to the astonishing conclusion that what Amir found inductively after refining, Strauss and Corbin introduced beforehand as an axiomatic paradigm. Likewise, Langenberg et al. introduced categories as a "paradigm" at the start. We must question such paradigms introduced beforehand.

The following, a description written by an observer, is an example of categorizing (translated from the original German text of Langenberg et al., 1992):

> I see a child, sitting in front of a xylophone, self-concentrated, and in a compulsive, monotonous way playing a children's song. The mother (the music therapist at the piano) tries to make contact to the child, and tries to lead the child to different, new tones, but fails, because the child is completely walled in, locked, unapproachable. The mother (or the educator) becomes impatient, annoyed, and expresses this halfheartedly. The child does not react to this, however; the mother-educator partially surrenders and for a while joins the child's play reluctantly but is not able to reach the child. I feel helplessness and a lot of sadness.

The categorization of this fragment is as follows (the chronological sequence is from the top to the bottom):

Quality 1	Quality 2	Quality 2A
Child is self-concentrated, monotonous		
Mother tries to make contact; tries to stimulate child to use new tones; fails		
Child is walled in, locked, unapproachable		
	Mother is impatient, annoyed; expresses this halfheartedly	
Child has no reaction		
Mother surrenders and joins; child is unapproachable		
	Mother is reluctant	I feel helplessness, sadness

Each individual description (of the observers, the music therapist, and the client) is categorized the same way.

Step 3: Generating Motifs

After categorization, every individual description is analyzed for content. As described by Mayring (1990), this involves using omissions (statements that appear more than once are omitted), generalizations (statements that are implied by more abstract statements are left out), selections (central statements are retained unchanged), and concentrations (related statements from various places in the text are brought together as a whole). The result is a set of concepts for every individual description. The next step is a second content analysis in which the concepts of all the individual descriptions are cross-analyzed. Similar statements in the different texts are underlined and, by means of group discussion, integrated and coded into more abstract categories called motifs. In the case described above, Langenberg et al. worked with five observers, the client, and the music therapist; here, the observations of only two observers are shown:

Motifs	Observer 1	Observer 2
Child	Child	Goblin
Isolation	Walled in	Mine-gallery
Rhythm	Monotonous	Stone mason's
Maturity	Mother	Chief goblin
Urging	Stimulating	Urging to work faster
Indulging	Trying to contact	
Impotence	Unapproachable	Not knowing the reason
Spent cartridge		Artificial/alienated
Annoyance	Annoyed impatience	Forceful
Violence		Threatening
Fear		

When we look at Observer 1's list above, we see that the word *locked* has been omitted from the list made in step 2 that included *walled in, locked,* and *unapproachable* (*self-concentrated, fails, no reaction, surrenders, joins, halfheartedly, reluctantly, helplessness,* and *sadness* were omitted, too). *Monotonous* has been generalized to *rhythm.* The world *child* has been selected as a general motif. In each motif, all the related fragments from different participants were concentrated. The selection of descriptions should be submitted to the criterion of "reliability"; whether each description correctly represents the phenomenon is a matter of "validity." Perhaps another research team would use *locked* and leave out *walled in. Locked,* of course, is really already represented in *walled in* and *unapproachable.* Other concepts that were left out, such as *helplessness* and *sadness,* are less well represented by the remaining concepts. The reason for this is that in this method, words (similar statements) are integrated into motifs found more than once in the transcripts of the different members of the research team. I favor working with a research panel, but we must note that the way motifs are constructed is reductive. Although there are different perspectives ("qualities," several data sources, perspectives of the research team members, descriptive and musical analyses), the motifs in the end represent homogenous, not multiple, perspectives because what does not fit into the motifs is left out. The research report gives no information about what decisions have been made and why.

Other remarks should be made, too. For example, we can look at the scheme vertically or horizontally. When looking vertically, we might ask why, for instance, *walled in* and *un-*

approachable were placed in separate categories. This splitting is understandable if we view *unapproachable* as referring more to the perspective of someone trying to reach someone else who is walled in. Nevertheless, another research group perhaps would have decided to place *walled in* and *unapproachable* in the same category or within subcategories of one general category. When looking at the scheme horizontally, we might ask why *mother* and *chief goblin* were generalized to *maturity*. Here, questioning "construct validity" is important. All the objections that we can make illustrate that this grid—as does all qualitative research—reflects the perspective of only one research team. The final question is not whether it can be done differently but whether it is credible enough to reflect the data.

Step 4: Finding the Analogy between Motifs and Music

In this step, the grid of motifs is connected to the musical analyses made by the musicians. This step resembles the search for "inside regulation" in morphological music therapy. In this step, the first musician describes the musical motif of the client as, for example tonica A, ostinato, not identical when repeated but not developing, having little melodic range, having the same timbre throughout, and having dynamics between p and mp. Because of the nonidentical repetitions, the second musician thinks there is a little bit of variation and development. The research team concludes that the musical analysis reflects the motifs of isolation, rhythm, impotence, fear, and annoyance.

Step 5: Finding the Analogy between Motifs and Psychodynamics

In this final step, the research team tries to connect the motifs of step 3 to the psychopathology of the client. This child had been emotionally frustrated and therefore had developed a pseudoautonomy, which remained in place when she achieved a lot—which in turn caused headaches—and did not make any mistakes. She could prevent mistakes only by being self-concentrated, not taking risks, and rejecting social challenges. At the same time, she experienced conflict because she wanted to free herself. The research team concluded from this that "freedom and restraint" were reflected and could be worked through in music therapy. A very important aspect of this research method is that the analogies between "experience," "music," and "psychopathology" are spelled out carefully. Since I am convinced that these concepts are central to music therapy (Smeijsters, 1996a), I believe this research method can be of great significance.

Step 6: Using the Multiple-Case Study

In this step, researchers investigate the possibility of making general statements by comparing case analyses. In the case discussed here, only two analyses of two sessions of one case have been made, so it is a "pilot study," and using multiple-case studies is a future possibility. The music therapist, the client, their intersection, and the improvisation are visualized as interlocking circles, much the way Kenny visualizes the "aesthetics" of the music therapist and the client, "the musical space" between them, and the "field of play."

I must make a final comment here about the quantity of work that must be invested in this method. One complete research project is used to analyze one single improvisation. It almost is impossible to use this method when researching a client's complete progress in music therapy. It can be used as a diagnostic tool, to analyze improvisations that seem to be very important, to construct analogies, or to compare improvisations from selected stages of therapy to indicate progress (for instance, at the beginning, halfway through, and at the end). By analyzing two sessions of one case, Langenberg et al. seem to advocate this application. As they themselves conclude, if the method is used that way, the criterion of "internal validity" needs special attention.

Chapter 9

RESEARCHERS AS
INSTRUMENTS

Ken Bruscia's contributions to qualitative research are enormous; they cannot be completely detailed here. His work can serve as a guide to the therapist who wishes to serve as his or her own researcher. First, we will discuss his contribution to the methodology of qualitative research, or the steps we should take when engaged in qualitative research. The procedures for planning and conducting a quantitative study have been systematically described. In qualitative research, however, descriptions of procedures are limited to a specific research method, and even then, they are not explicit. Therefore, an overall procedural tool, as described by Bruscia, can be helpful. Then, we will discuss Bruscia's qualitative research into modes of consciousness, and finally, we will discuss the criterion of "authenticity," which can guide qualitative research.

THE PROCESS OF
QUALITATIVE RESEARCH

Bruscia has provided a detailed framework for conducting qualitative research (Bruscia, 1995c, 1995d, 1995e). I will not repeat the entire framework here but will instead comment on several interesting aspects of it.

The qualitative researcher, according to Bruscia, is interested in unplanned, unmanipulated real-world settings. We might argue that the music therapy session is not a real-world setting. It is planned by the music therapist, and by using play forms and techniques, the music therapist manipulates. This is different from an experimental setting, however, because manipulations develop freely and are not limited by research interventions and free improvisation cannot be planned. In the natural therapy setting, music therapists constantly adjust their manipulations, but they are still manipulations. When a qualitative researcher supports the privilege of the music therapist to deciding which manipulations should be used, then the qualitative researcher, too, is manipulating, or even "experimenting" along with the music therapist. We even could hold the view—as was described in previous chapters—that the music therapist's way of thinking is just like that of the researcher who wants to know how things work. At this, I can almost hear some of my colleagues raising their voices in criticism that this is a positivistic way of thinking, but I think we should remember that music therapists make use of techniques and play forms that benefit the client and monitor the process's development when they introduce new therapeutic measures. They do not necessarily believe in naive cause and effect; nevertheless, they hope that their (musical) behavior contributes to their clients' progress. What I am saying is that music therapy is not an experiment because the process can develop freely and variables are not held constant, but the reflection of the music therapist resembles somehow the experimental idea. Qualitative research methods like member checking are manipulative, too. I would say there always is manipulation, it can be flexible like in natural treatment and qualitative research linked to that treatment, or it can be fixed like in experimental research.

Bruscia believes qualitative research should not be narrowed down to mere experience, calling events, experiences, materials, and people possible research phenomena. This is a very important point. Researchers often recommend a qualitative study design because it can describe the experience that they see as the essence of music therapy, thus sometimes making other phenomena appear less important. I think it is the combination of different phenomena that is important. For instance, experience should be linked to musical processes (as, for example, in works by Tüpker and Langenberg and in the principle of analogy), because without this link, we cannot prove that the essence of music therapy also is musical.

So that you will want to read Bruscia's chapters in Wheeler (Bruscia, 1995c, 1995d, 1995e), here is a summary of all the issues he handles. First, he discusses the steps in establishing a focus and purpose:

1. Select a topic:
   A. Choose between discipline topics or professional topics (for instance, treatment or training).
   B. Narrow down the topic.
   C. Choose types of clients or therapists.
   D. Choose the kind of research.
2. Target phenomena:
   A. Observable events (for instance, actions)
   B. Covert experiences (feelings, images, thoughts, and so on)
   C. Resulting materials (for example, a taped improvisation)
   D. People
3. Define the scope:
   A. A single instance or occurrence (for instance, one improvisation)
   B. Multiple occurrences belonging to one data source (idiographic; for instance, several improvisations by one person or group)
   C. Comparing several data sources (nomothetic; for instance, improvisations of different individuals)
4. Define purposes:
   A. Holistic description (additive description of everything of significance)
   B. Essence (looking for the characteristics by reducing various parts of data to what is similar or by systematically imagining how the essence of a phenomenon changes when elements are eliminated from it)
   C. Analysis (discovering patterns, recurrences, categories, types, themes)
   D. Theory building (formulating constructs, principles, or conceptual schemes beyond the data and on a higher level than analysis)
   E. Interpretation (discerning deeper structures, searching for underlying appearances and symbols, applying existing theories)

F. Re-creation (reproducing an interaction and empathizing with the participant)
G. Critique (evaluating the data)
H. Self-exploration (gaining firsthand personal understanding by participating, with the researcher as a data source)

Looking at this outline makes classifying qualitative research methods easy. For instance, Langenberg's method focuses on treatment of clients; experiences of clients, therapists, and observers; materials (musical score); one or two improvisations; analysis (motifs); and interpretation (linking motifs with personality and psychopathology). The two techniques used to identify essence are taken from phenomenology. The second one is phenomenological variation, or eidetic reduction. Phenomenological researchers then can be classified as concentrating on treatment of clients, experiences of clients and therapists, a single instance, and essence.

Just looking at the purpose shows that Amir's search for meaningful moments by developing core categories and subcategories falls into the category analysis. Bruscia's research into modes of consciousness is an attempt to build a theory (described later in this chapter). Morphological methodology, in which musical patterns are conceived as symbols of the client's "life method" and explained with concepts from morphological psychology, can be classified as interpretation. Looking for analogies in musical processes and exploring existing theories of psychopathology to which they can be linked is interpretative, too (as, for instance, in my own research method, described later in this book).

Examples of self-exploration can be found in studies in which the researcher acts as therapist or as a participant during the session: Aigen, when making audiovisual tapes in "Here We Are in Music" (1995a), was a participant, and Bruscia, in "Modes of Consciousness" (1995b), was the therapist. Bruscia suggests several procedural steps:

1. **Focus:** Here, make all the decisions outlined above. The focus is open-ended and may shift.
2. **Contextualize:** Identify the different contexts: yourself; your professional framework, interpersonal con-

texts, previous research, theory, and practice; the setting (naturalistic or artificial); participants' personal context; the sociopolitical context.

3. **Design the study:**
   A. Determine the type of cases (understand several aspects of one person or one aspect of several people), the range of data (one instance, one participant, or several participants), and the type of setting (for example, natural, observable in the present).
   B. Select samples (typical, deviant, or controversial). This is an ongoing process. In successive sampling, take previous data into account and consider participants' potential strengths.
   C. Select the type of data comparisons: intraindividual/ interindividual, intraphenomenal/interphenomenal (for instance: between events or between event and experience), intramodal/intermodal (only music or music and other media), intraobserver/ interobserver, intramusical/intermusical (within one piece or between several pieces), intraverbal/ interverbal (within one narrative or between several narratives).
   D. Determine the researcher's roles (engaging participants, coresearchers, and observers; participating him- or herself?), the participants' roles (observed in a naturalistic setting, taking part in the research process?), the therapist's roles (engaging the participant, collecting data, evaluating him- or herself, serving as coresearcher, consultant, or participant?), and the consultant's roles (participant, coresearcher, therapist, assistant?).
   E. Choose how participants will be engaged (improvising, listening, re-creating, imaging, drawing).
   F. Submit the research design to a commission of ethics for review.
4. **Gather Data:** Use observation (events), interviews/ self-reports/(self)-dialogues (experiences) to create/archive/ analyze (materials).

5. **Record:** Preserve the music therapy session (by notes, audiovisual tapes, transcripts of tapes).
6. **Process Data:** Organize, analyze, or interpret the data. Which techniques are used here depends strongly on the type of qualitative research that has been chosen—grounded theory, phenomenology, morphology, or naturalistic inquiry. Bruscia gives a summary of almost all the possible techniques. Here are the most important ones that can be linked to the qualitative research methods described in this book:
   A. Get a sense of the whole.
   B. Create segments of meaningful units.
   C. Eliminate redundant or irrelevant units.
   D. Code each unit.
   E. Use related units to describe the whole phenomenon or search for the essence of a phenomenon by comparing several units.
   F. Analyze deeper relationships and connect units by asking if one is an attribute of, cause of, type of, stage of, means for, or reason for another.
   G. Regroup units from different contexts into one category.
   H. Synthesize by relating regroupings of data and developing a higher level of abstraction.
   I. Go back to the data and ground the developed constructs in the original data.
   J. Interpret by uncovering hidden aspects of the data, giving meaning to the data, and constructing the data within the framework of a theory.
   K. Theorize: develop a theory that goes beyond the data.
   L. Experience by personally interacting with the data.
   M. Re-create by musically imitating or drawing to the data.
   N. Monitor trustworthiness.
7. **Communicate:**
   A. Choose the goals of communication.
   B. Choose a unique outline of the report.

    C. Choose the medium and type of language: written text or recording, scientific or metaphoric language, third person ("the researcher") or first person ("I").

  8. **Appraise:** Continuously evaluate and refine every aspect of the research process:

    A. Revise the direction of research during the research process (being open to failure, success, and doubts).

    B. Establish trustworthiness (credibility, applicability, consistency and neutrality).

Some further clarification should be made because sometimes different steps refer to the same aspects. For instance, determining the setting is part of contextualizing, but it is also of designing the study and the role of participants. It also seems that previous choices determine subsequent choices. When, for example, the researcher chooses to focus on only one instance (step 1), this means that he or she limits the scope to one event, to a single experience of one person, to one object, or to one individual or group through a single event, experience, or object. Then, intraindividual (several examples of an experience of the same person), interindividual (experiences of several persons), intraphenomenal (several events), interphenomenal (an event and experience of the event), intramodal (several musical pieces), intraobserver (several observations), intermusical (comparisons between two or more pieces), and interverbal (comparisons between several narratives) focuses are impossible. Choosing one instance as the study's scope then leaves the following possibilities:

- Intermodal (such as music and words connected to music)
- Interobserver (observations of several researchers)
- Intramusical (comparisons within one piece of music)
- Intraverbal (comparisons within one narrative).

Thus, the procedural decisions that must be made are not independent from each other but form a interlinked pattern. These distinct patterns describe distinct qualitative research designs for gathering data, as Bruscia points out. A self-report is commonly used when the focus is on experience, and musical analysis is linked to materials.

It is almost impossible to follow all the guidelines in one research design. I think researchers should try to develop research designs that are consistent and then compare them to Bruscia's scheme to see what is missing and why. As an example, I will try here to describe my own research design within Bruscia's framework: My professional background is that of a social scientist and psychomusicologist trained not only as a quantitative researcher but also as a humanistic therapist. This means that I am acquainted with positivistic and phenomenological thought. As a quantitative researcher, I am motivated to try to obtain nonbiased findings, yet as a phenomenologist, I know that human beings and experiences cannot be reduced to standardized measurements and that I need my subjectivity to understand life. I am aware that having these two different foci sometimes causes me trouble.

In my early research, I concentrated on philosophical research in musicology (technology in music of the twentieth century). From an analytic point of view, you might say that I criticized technology so strongly because on an unconscious level I longed for a universal technique that would help me influence my environment and lessen my existential anxiety. I know—and this is very conscious—that I had to deal with the idea that I could predict and influence human behavior by the techniques I used. I had to counteract a personal tendency to think in variables—"this causes that."

Then I did some research in music psychology (the connotations and functions of music). For the last 8 years, I have concentrated fully on research in music therapy, mostly qualitative, but incidentally quantitative. I generally hold that theory should be developed out of practice, but when I am doing research, I use existing concepts if they fit the specific case. I prefer my research setting to be naturalistic: everything looks like a normal therapy session. There are several artificial aspects, however: clients know that videotapes are made, that they will be studied, and that an observer is watching from behind a one-way screen. I always obtain informed consent to tape clients, using a one-way screen only when clients do not mind.

The participants' personal context is that they live at home but are treated by a psychotherapist once a week. The psychotherapist refers the clients to music therapy. Patients take part in both psychotherapy and music therapy voluntarily. In The Netherlands, music therapy is not paid for by health-insurance companies. At the Music Therapy Laboratory of Hogeschool van Arnhem (Nijmegen, The Netherlands), treatment is free to clients; treatment and research are paid for by training program funds because the treatment and research result in better-trained teachers serving as music therapists and in the development of case studies that can be of use in the training program (possible only when agreed to by clients).

As a researcher, I try to understand several aspects of one person and concentrate on one participant. There is no selection of samples because clients are referred when music therapy seems to be indicated. Sometimes clients are not accepted when it is thought that their disturbances are severe enough to warrant treatment in an inpatient institution. The types of data comparisons I use are intraindividual, intraphenomenal (between events), interphenomenal (between event and experience), intramodal (only music), sometimes intermodal (between music and, for instance, drawing), intraobserver and interobserver, intramusical (within one improvisation), intermusical (within several improvisations), intraverbal (within one narrative), and interverbal (between several narratives). The interpersonal context is characterized by an equal relationship between me as senior researcher, the registered music therapist who provides the treatment, and the observer. The music therapist and the observer are invited to be coresearchers. As a researcher, I do not participate in treatment myself, but when possible, I communicate with the clients outside treatment sessions. Most of the time, however, there is no communication between us. The observer does not communicate with the client, either. Clients are engaged by improvising and listening.

Research outside the Music Therapy Laboratory is reviewed by the psychiatric clinic's commission of ethics. The research conducted in the Music Therapy Laboratory is reviewed by the research fund administrators. I gather data by observation, interview, self-report, and analysis of materials. The music therapy sessions are recorded in notes, on audiovisual tapes, and in tape transcripts. I organize, analyze, and interpret data. I select meaningful units when I describe focus points and eliminate redundant or irrelevant units. I code each meaningful unit by a short title. I regroup units from different contexts into one category, aiming at a higher level of abstraction. I ground constructs in the original data and related units when I use them to describe the whole phenomenon. I analyze and connect units of assessment and treatment, checking whether one is an attribute, cause, or stage of another. I uncover hidden aspects of the data and connect them to the framework of a theory or develop a new theory that goes beyond the data.

I establish trustworthiness through member checking, peer debriefing, and repeated analysis, a detailed study that makes it possible to replicate the chain of evidence. Special qualitative aspects of my research method are open coding, hypothesis generation, triangulation, negative case analysis, dialectical roles, and musical analysis. I continuously evaluate and refine every aspect of the research process. Looking for side effects, disturbances, and catalysts is my way of being open to failure and doubts. My main goal in communication is to stimulate the music therapist to look for side effects, disturbances, and catalysts and to present some guidelines that can be used as hypotheses for treatment and research.

In the beginning of any research project, the report and article outlines resemble traditional structures, but gradually, the structure becomes freer, changing a little bit every time. I use written text as my report format and include metaphorical language only when one of the participants uses of it. Although I use the first person here to describe the research process, I cannot do so when presenting particular research findings, because they are the result of the research team's interaction.

From this description of my own research method, we can see that Bruscia's criteria can be of great help in describing what we are doing—it can be used not only to categorize research but also to describe methods.

Sometimes interpreting research findings is difficult, and this is where we should spend more time. This brings us to another kind of self-inquiry: as a means of research, which Bruscia also describes. Researchers using this method explore their own attitudes, feelings, and thoughts. Here, such concepts as "subjectivity" and "countertransference," discussed in earlier chapters, take on a research context. There are several stances we can take. First, self-inquiry is necessary to detect our own biases as researchers. This means that we should be aware of when our own life experiences are projected onto the client's. The second view is much more positive: that researchers' feelings, thoughts, and so on can contribute to understanding clients. Understanding other people—feeling what they feel—is possible only if we feel our own feelings. Excluding subjectivity would be very short-sighted, but as we have argued earlier, how can we know whether subjectivity is biased? That question, however, is not the one at hand here.

Bruscia sees an analogy between finding a track in life and keeping a focus in research. Indeed, because qualitative researchers do not follow a prepared route, they are prone to doubts about decisions, prestige, and so forth. As I write this, I remember my own struggles as a researcher, my insecurity about the interpretations and decisions I made, my sensitivity to colleagues and critics. I gradually became convinced that as qualitative researchers, we should try to be open with ourselves and reflect on our thoughts and feelings about our studies. We should bring to the conscious level those personal motives that might direct our research. This takes courage and requires that we trust ourselves, but showing ourselves as people with insecurities and doubts is more "valid" than trying to rationalize findings in an impersonal clear picture that attempts to disguise weaknesses. If we accept our own doubts, then others will trust our work.

MODES OF CONSCIOUSNESS

When using Guided Imagery and Music (GIM) with a client, Bruscia was struck by the fact that his own consciousness constantly moved toward the client and away from him. In a first attempt at understanding this, he used the analogy between shifts of consciousness and modulation in music. Consciousness, for him, is like music: it can be in one mode, in transition between modes, in different modes, or in no mode. His research questions were: How did I do it? How is it possible to be there? How was I there? Aigen (1995c) describes this type of research as hermeneutic because there is a constant exchange between phenomena and theory in the effort to understand the phenomena. The hermeneutic cycle describes a dialectical process in which the meaning of the parts is determined by foreknowledge of the whole and the knowledge of the whole is continuously corrected and deepened by the increased knowledge of the parts. There is a constant re-evaluation of the whole and the parts (see Rowan and Reason, 1991).

The meaning of Bruscia's research into the modes of consciousness is twofold. First, it can be seen as an example of phenomenological and introspective research methods because it focuses on the therapist's experience and is done by means of introspection of the therapist himself. The therapist is his own researcher. There is no interviewing another therapist, no obtaining impressions experienced by panel members who listen to music therapy sessions. Although it would have been possible for Bruscia to study the topic of what happens inside himself by being interviewed by another researcher, it seems clear that he is closer to his internal experiences by serving as his own researcher.

Qualitative researchers often say that the researcher is the instrument, meaning that the researcher's thoughts, feelings, images, and intuitions are the most important data in the research process. In Bruscia's case, we could say that the researcher is the instrument and researches his own instrument. This brings us to the second meaning of this research: it gives us insight in what is happening when the researcher is the instrument. In positivistic research, introspection has always been suspect, but the claims of positivistic research are different. Establishing "truth" in positivistic research means that there has to be the possibility that someone else can replicate and verify the findings. Let me illustrate with an example from religion: a revelation never can be "scientific" in a positivistic sense, because it is purely personal and subjective. Nobody else can verify the perceptions of the person who had the revelation. But when "truth" is interpreted differently, the positivistic argument fails. When we focus on "experience," it can be true even when it is not true in the positivistic sense; that is, an experience is true simply because it is there. The way someone experiences "reality" is a subjective reality in itself: that he or she experiences it that way is "true." It is not important whether this experience corresponds with something outside his or her experience, but it is important that he or she experienced it. When a researcher tries to experience how he or she is experiencing, nobody can replicate his or her experience of that experience. The benefit is personal: it is important that he or she is able to make sense of that experience. This does not mean that the process is totally intrasubjective. There is the possibility of replication, but not positivistic replication. It is impossible for somebody else to replicate my experience because it is mine, but it is possible to experience my own experience, to make a personal "theory" of it. By comparing my "personal theory" of my own experience with someone else's "personal theory," I can compare my experience with someone else's.

Let us look at Bruscia's theory of experience. He makes a distinction between three experiential spaces: the client's world, his own personal world, and his world as a therapist. Further, there are four levels of experiencing, taken from the work of Carl Jung: the sensory level, the affective level, the level of reflection, and the intuitive level. To illustrate this, he gives the transcript of the opening session with a young man with acquired immunodeficiency syndrome (AIDS). He uses the following codes:

- C = client's world
- P = therapist's personal world
- T = therapist's world
- 1 = sensory
- 2 = affective
- 3 = reflective
- 4 = intuitive

In GIM, he uses the tape *Creativity III*. It starts with Wilhelm Richard Wagner's "Siegfried Idyll." The client, Tom, experiences the image of resting in a meadow, on a sunny day, surrounded by flowers. This dialogue follows:

Dialogue	Modes of Consciousness
Tom: I feel bones down there. They seem to be cracked into several pieces. I found a skull. It's broken in two. The edges are real jagged.	**C2:** I can feel him getting nervous about what he's digging up. **P2:** I don't want this skeleton to be him. **T1:** His body is tensing.
Ken: How are you feeling? **Tom:** Confused. Why am I digging up bones in such a beautiful place?	**T1:** He has a mischievous look on his face. **P2:** I really enjoy his sense of humor. **T4:** I think he is going to blame me (or my selection of the music) for his images (as he has done previously). **T3:** Give him options so that he can take responsibility for what's happening.
Ken: Is there something you'd rather be doing in this meadow? **Tom:** (Smiling) No . . . now that I've started this, I'm curious about these bones.	**C3:** Tom knows that my question was an attempt to avoid his accusations. Or he may have the impression that I think he is "chicken." **T3:** Don't get into the transference. He needs to gather more information about the bones.
Ken: How many bones are there? **Tom:** Enough to make a person. . . . I am arranging them on the ground.	**C1:** I can imagine a skeleton forming.
Tom: I wonder if the bones are me. But when I look around, I get flashes of this person being stoned to death.	**T3+4:** Wasn't Mary Magdalen being stoned for promiscuity when Christ redeemed her? I wonder if Tom is digging up guilt over the past. **P2:** The music is sad. **P4:** This scene is going to bring him great sadness. **P2:** I wish I could spare him this. **C2:** I feel his vulnerability. **T3:** I may be reacting more emotionally than he is, and in different sensory channels. I'm hear-feel and he's in a visual mode. He needs more vivid visual information.

Several aspects of Bruscia's modes of consciousness are more subjective, and several are less so. For instance, "I can feel him getting nervous" and "His body is tensing" are empathic and observational, whereas "I don't want this" reflects a personal experience. The first type of quotations normally are used by music therapists. What is new is the personal dimension of the therapist and the alternation between the modes. It seems as if the modes of consciousness could be differentiated further. For example, "I think he is going to blame me" differs from "Give him options so that he can take responsibility for what's happening" and "Don't get into the transference." There is the difference not only between intuition and reflection but also between observing and choosing strategies. The latter should be an important part of research reports. Often, a lot of data are gathered, but the reflections of the music therapist and what he or she planned to do and why are neglected.

The important role of intuition is illustrated by the story of Mary Magdalen. It is the therapist's association when the client brings up "being stoned to death." By associating Mary Magdalen with the client's image, the therapist immediately has an entire group of thoughts on sexual behavior, guilt, punishment, and death. Although this association is classified as T3+4, the story of Mary Magdalen and the thoughts resulting from remembering it come from the therapist's background. Someone who is not familiar with the Bible would not make this link. The interpretation of being stoned to death is determined by the therapist's association. Perhaps this should be coded as P, also.

After this analysis, Bruscia concludes that these constructs cannot reflect adequately his experience. According to Bruscia, three other categories should be included: personal positions within the client's world, parameters of the client–therapist relationship, and media of transportation. Each category in turn contains several subcategories:

- Personal positions in the client's world: fusion (C = P), accommodation (C/P), assimilation (P/C), differentiation (C/= P), objectification (C→P or C→T)
- Parameters of the C–T relationship: transference (TT), countertransference (XT), authentic (AT)
- Media of transportation: altered states of consciousness (ASC), music (MUS), imagery (IMA), physical interaction (PHY), verbal interaction (VRB)

Then he uses these new constructs in the analysis of a further transcript of the session:

Dialogue	Modes of Consciousness
Tom: I feel like I have to forgive them all. **Ken:** Is that what you would like to do?	**AT3/VRB:** I wonder why he said "have to." **P1+2:/MUS:** The Schumann is over (I feel relieved) and **AT1+3/MUS:** Elgar's "Sospiri" has begun. It is slow and mournful and is ideal for supporting where Tom seems to be headed. **P3:** I do not have the intense associations to this piece.
Tom: Yes.	**AT3/IMA:** This may be a good opportunity to get him into the scene, so that he can stop being a split-off observer.
Ken: Is it safe for you to step into the scene now and try? **Tom:** Yes . . . it's okay now. I feel like I am becoming one of the men who stoned him. I am sitting on the ground with them . . . next to the dead man. Some of us are crying. It feels as if we are really no different from the man.	**P/C2/IMA:** This scene feels like a viewing or wake. **AT3:** The music seems to be grieving for us all. **AT3/IMA:** It seems significant that he did not enter the scene as himself and that he became one of the penitent ones who wants forgiveness.
Ken: No different? **Tom:** No . . . we all die with regrets.	**P/C2+3/IMA:** I feel like he wants to confess his own regrets before he confronts his own death.
Ken: Does everyone there have regrets? **Tom:** No . . . some of the people are still angry and are walking away. **Ken:** Do you want to say anything to them? **Tom:** Yes: "Wait a minute! Why have you done this to him?" (Resumes crying)	**AT3/IMA:** Is he splitting again? **C=P2/IMA:** I feel Tom's confusion and sorrow. I feel his identification with the man. **P3:** Tom is finally standing up for the man and perhaps for himself.
Tom: They're telling me: "He was guilty—he was bad." **Ken:** "But what did he do?" **Tom:** "Nothing . . . he was innocent—he was just different."	**P/C4/VRB:** Being gay makes Tom different and innocent. **AT3:** But in Tom's heart, this innocence makes him guilty, and this difference makes him bad.

As in the first excerpt, codes other than the one Bruscia used are also appropriate. For instance, the music therapist, reflecting that "This may be a good opportunity. . .", at that point is also in the therapist's world (T). What is also interesting is that the music therapist uses *splitting* twice. If the generation of categories is "open," then maybe in this case, there should be a category called "splitting." It might be useful to compare the music therapist's own analysis with the analysis made by someone else so that constructs can be clarified and adjusted. Until this point in the session, Bruscia had concentrated on "where" the music therapist was moving. So that the "how" and "when" can be included, he finally proposes adding two more categories: "freedom of access" and "timing." If we summarize this research method, we can distinguish—but not separate—several steps:

1. Experiencing several sessions
2. Generating constructs from these experiences
3. Experiencing new sessions
4. Analyzing the verbal transcripts with the constructs
5. Generating supplementary constructs
6. Experiencing new sessions
7. Analyzing the verbal transcripts with the constructs

. . . and so on.

When we analyze the constructs Bruscia uses—the four levels of experience and such words as *fusion, accommodation,* and *assimilation*—we see that they are influenced by theory (Carl Jung, Gestalt, Jean Piaget). Thus, Bruscia's method is not grounded theory, and although experience is important, it is not phenomenology. It is important to ask whether the constructs categorize experience, or if the constructs were used *because* they reflect experience. Although this research method takes into consideration the experiential space of the client's world, the music therapist/researcher fully concentrated on his experiences of that world. Because there is a lot of talking, the client's experience surfaces, too, but the analytical method concentrates on the researcher's experience of the client's experience, and not on the client's experience as such. Of course, this was the topic of this research study, so this criticism seems unjustified. I only want to make clear that this research method differs from other qualitative research methods in which the experiences of the client, observers, and research team members are equally reflected.

The same difference holds true for the music. There is no independent description of the musical process, only the therapist's experience of it. How do we use this method when there is an improvisation? Perhaps there would then be no verbal sequence that could be studied. To work around this, the researcher might supplement the dialogue with descriptions of the actions and surroundings (for example, the musical process), as in the script for a scene in a play.

AUTHENTICITY

The value and trustworthiness of findings have been discussed in music therapy for several years now (see, for instance, Aigen, 1995c, and previous chapters in this book). In a chapter on authenticity, Bruscia (1996a) refers to Guba and Lincoln (1989), who, to ensure research authenticity, have added four criteria to those they set forth in 1985 (credibility, dependability, transferability, and confirmability):

- *Ontological authenticity*: The inquiry leads to enlarged personal constructions.
- *Educative authenticity*: The inquiry leads to improved understanding of others' constructions.
- *Catalytic authenticity*: The inquiry leads to action.
- *Tactical authenticity*: The inquiry empowers people to act.

The question of authenticity is linked to values. Since the work of Horkheimer and Adorno (1981) and the start of what is called the "positivism war," it has become clear that the Weberian ideal of "value-free" research can never really exist. Therefore, many—Aigen (1996a), for example—have stressed that researchers should communicate their values, not hide them. The issue of authenticity also makes clear why member checking is so important: it guarantees that that research is of value to those it concerns. Authenticity should be of concern to every researcher. We must question who benefits from our research. Is it us? Is it our clients, the professional community, the institution? Inauthenticity occurs when researchers want to succeed and therefore concentrate on their own theorizing and not on the subject. In a society in which success is the only thing that counts, this inauthenticity can easily creep in. From my own experience as a researcher, I can assure you that we all must be aware of it and fight it or, as Aigen suggests, communicate about it.

The same holds true for music therapists. Music therapists who are forced to show effects may be forced into inauthenticity: they may feel they must elevate their own status. They are working not for the client's benefit but for their own. Professional interests should not interfere with research and treatment, and research and treatment should be extremely open, which means researchers must stand ready not only to claim success but also to admit failure. Bruscia's concern is not reflected by Guba and Lincoln's criteria; for him, it arose from his own struggles as a researcher and from the inauthenticity he perceived in other researchers. It comes close to the proverbial researcher who wants to verify his theory and neglects divergent data.

Bruscia defines *authenticity* as bringing into one's awareness whatever is possible to bring into it and acting in a way consistent with what is in that awareness. From this, we can deduce two possible forms of inauthenticity: (1) not bringing something into awareness and (2) not acting consistent with what is in awareness. Bruscia further defines *authenticity* as an intrasubjective standard and an ongoing process. *Intrasubjective* means that researchers must themselves protect their authenticity. An indication of authenticity is when, according to Bruscia, the researcher is convinced that he or she can trust him- or herself. This intrasubjectivity is a difficult issue. When I am inauthentic and fooling myself, then asking myself if I am authentic is subject to the same foolishness. When discussing introspection, we could argue that something is true because it is experienced as being true. When a researcher wants to be authentic, is it enough for him or her to say, however, "I am authentic when I experience myself as authentic?" There should be more than a feeling of self-trust to indicate authenticity. Let us follow Bruscia's ideas further and see if there is. The various authenticity issues we will discuss here can be summarized as follows:

1. Is what I am doing therapy or research? Am I seeking insight for the sake of the client under study or for the sake of other clients?
2. Is what I am doing empirical research, developing a theory based on other research findings, or writing a personal narrative without including new data?
3. When doing qualitative research, do I have a belief system congruent with the paradigm?
4. Am I conducting research with a focus?
5. Am I bringing into awareness my countertransference as a researcher?
6. Have I chosen a research method appropriate for the phenomenon?
7. Am I picking up unexpected or contradictory findings?
8. Am I communicating about my research in such a way it that is clear to the reader that I am responsible for the choices made and am not hiding anything?

I wonder if the differentiation between therapy and research should be made only because of the music therapist's intention. The client's experience is very important, too. If the client feels like a guinea pig when therapy and research are combined, then there is a serious problem. The client experiences the situation as inauthentic.

There are several authentic links between treatment and research, however. First, research can be done within the setting of a therapy practice to stimulate the development of a unique context. Then there is no "out there": the research benefits the client alone. Second, the client may experience the research process as additional attention contributing to his or her treatment process. In both of these situations, there is no conflict of intentions for the music therapist/researcher. He or she can say, "I am researching because of therapy" or "I want to better understand you and my clinical understanding of you [the researcher's point of view], for your sake [the therapist's point of view]."

Apart from the matter of intention there is another difference between therapy and research: working as a therapist is different from working as a researcher. When the music therapist is also the researcher, one person is living in two worlds, and the roles of therapist and researcher can be confused. The easy way out of this dilemma—splitting the roles of music therapist

and researcher—evokes other problems (see my own research
method, discussed earlier in this chapter).

Critics of qualitative research often argue that it is nonscientific. It would be a mistake to fend off this statement by
labeling it as "positivistic." The truth is that qualitative research
sometimes *is* nonscientific, as when what the therapist is doing as
a therapist is called research. Bruscia's issue of intention can be
viewed in light of this contention. When a case study is presented as
research, session notes that originally served therapy now are used
as research data. Then there is confusion of intention because during
the treatment process, the therapist perhaps did not intend to do
research, and during therapy he and the client did not think in terms
of research. Acknowledging that what you do is research is a matter
of integrity and ethics, but acknowledgment is only part of the story.
Because it was not research in the first place, the research
requirements cannot be fulfilled. Bruscia addressed this point by
including the word *systematic* in his definition of *research*:

- An inquiry into the unknown
- A systematic gathering of data
- Self-monitored with regard to integrity
- Context- and client-specific
- Relevant to a community of researchers

When you decide afterward that treatment is "research," then you
failed to do a systematic gathering of data. In Bruscia's definition,
we should question the criteria of relevance because this is a
matter of paradigm. As the examples given by Kühn (1975)
illustrate, research findings often are dismissed as irrelevant
because they do not support the paradigm in vogue at the time,
but after time passes and the popular paradigm changes, they
may then be considered very relevant.

The third authenticity issue—whether the researcher
holds a belief system consistent with the research paradigm
used—leads to the conclusion that a researcher who is doing
qualitative research should adopt the belief system belonging to
that method: that there is no absolute truth, that there are no
immutable laws, but multiple perspectives. The quantitative and
qualitative belief systems cannot be combined at the same time.
Bruscia writes that quantitative and qualitative types of data can
be gathered at different times; I would like to add that this can be

done by the same person at different times. I am convinced that it is possible, as a researcher, to switch between the qualitative and quantitative research paradigms without being inauthentic as a person. I do not see as self-evident the conclusion that because of the impossibility of combining the two belief systems logically it also is impossible for one researcher to use both the qualitative and quantitative paradigms. It *is* possible to use qualitative data within the quantitative belief system and qualitative data within the quantitative belief system.

Bruscia's fourth authenticity criteria—acting on the basis of whether one has a focus—means that when I am interviewing, for instance, having a focus means that I conduct the interview within the focus. I come close to manipulation when I let research participants think there is no focus when there is. Again, this is a matter of ethics. It is my experience that focus points do change in qualitative research. There are transitional stages in which the old focal points still exist but the new data point to new distinct focal points. Because of this, all the data should be recorded equally at every point of the research process. Only then it is possible that the research fits the therapeutic process and a shift of focus can take place. Researchers should take into account that because of their personalities and professional backgrounds, they will never be completely unfocused, even when all data are included. There are no data about which researchers do not have personal theories.

Researchers' countertransferences bring their own biographies into the picture. Therapists sometimes become therapists because they experienced personal problems and by curing clients, they are trying to cure themselves. Researchers sometimes do research because they want to focus on problems that are relevant in their own lives. As researchers, we should ask ourselves why we are doing particular research? Are we interested in our own needs? Do we handle research topics as we handle our own lives? Do we want to be successful? The latter easily can lead to inauthenticity, in which a qualitative researcher uses member checking to fulfill the requirements of the methods but hopes there will be no corrections to his or her report. On one hand, the researcher appreciates criticism, but on the other, he or she cannot stand it and perhaps feels insecure or even angry about it. This could be called paradigmatic inauthenticity. In quantitative research, the researcher does not use member checking to develop multiple perspectives but develops a theory for which he or she is responsible.

Being open to unexpected and contradictory findings is to me one of the most important criteria of authenticity. In the qualitative research method I developed, I use such concepts such as side effects, disturbances, and catalysts to intentionally look for phenomena I did not expected in the first place. Member checking, peer debriefing, and dialectical discussions are means to enhance the possibility that unexpected findings will arise. Naming the unexpected things—and the disappointments—in your research report will prevent you from hiding something. Here, countertransference can get in the way of integrity. The music therapist/researcher who wants to be successful will avoid reporting failures, although for science, failure is as important as success.

Bruscia criticizes researchers who do not carefully select their methods, who say that their methods are "determined solely by the phenomenon" or "prescribed by the paradigm." Bruscia brings up a very important issue here: not everything a person does is qualitative research. His two rules—that the method should be appropriate to the phenomenon and that methods are shaped by reciprocal interactions between the phenomenon, the participants, and the researcher—can be extended. Although the qualitative paradigm does not determine the method, there is a collection of methods and techniques from which the qualitative researcher should choose to meet the research criteria of internal validity (credibility), reliability (dependability), external validity (transferability), and objectivity (confirmability). Researchers are free to select method, adjust them to phenomena, and develop them through reciprocal interaction; however, what they use should belong to the stock of qualitative research methodology. Anything else cannot be considered research.

Does following Bruscia's recommendations ensure that we avoid the two types of inauthenticity (not bringing something into awareness and not acting consistent with what is in our awareness)? I would say the second type is easy to avoid. When something is in your awareness, then you are conscious of it and you will be conscious, too, of when you neglect it. The first type of inauthenticity is problematic. When, because of unconscious defenses, not everything is reaching my awareness, I still might trust myself and feel authentic. Despite Bruscia's claim of an intrapersonal solution, researchers can be sure that they are not fooling themselves only when they use such interpersonal methods as member checking and peer debriefing.

Chapter 10

CONSTRUCTING
THE CLIENT'S EXPERIENCE

Ken Aigen, a music therapist and director of research at the Nordoff-Robbins Music Therapy Clinic of New York University, has made significant contributions to music therapy research theory and developed his own qualitative research method. In this chapter, we will first discuss some of his most important theories and then review his research method.

MASTER CLINICIANS AS RESEARCHERS

Aigen's approach is based on the naturalistic paradigm, of which some fundamentals (see Lincoln and Guba, 1985) are as follows:

- Realities are multiple constructs.
- Knower and known are interactive.
- Only time- and context-bound idiographic hypotheses are possible.
- It is impossible to distinguish between cause and effect.
- Inquiry is value-bound.

One of his most striking statements (1993) is not only that master clinicians should be interviewed but that they are researchers. This is a completely new perspective: Clinicians' experiences and reflections on those experiences become "validated" as research data. I agree that the analysis of music therapy should include master clinicians' experiences, but the statement is difficult to follow. First, what is a "master" clinician? Second, does the inclusion of "master" clinicians automatically mean that we should abandon quantitative research methods?

I will try to answer these questions. First, is a "master" clinician anyone with more than a couple years' clinical experience? Aigen refers to Nordoff and Robbins (1977) as master clinicians. Not only did they work as music therapists for years, but they developed theoretical constructs by analyzing many hours' worth of tapes. These clinicians adopted a research attitude when doing their work, taping and then analyzing sessions. This makes them special, and therefore Aigen's statement perhaps should be changed to: "Experienced clinicians who analyze their work regularly and systematically can be called master clinicians." This alone is not enough, however, because what counts—what ensures scientific trustworthiness—is the way they do the analysis. We need to know what "system" they use and we should be able to replicate their systematic analysis. This means the definitive statement would be: "Experienced clinicians who analyze their work regularly and systematically can be called master clinicians. If they make sound methodological reports about their analyses, they can be called researchers."

To the second question, we could answer that researching master clinicians' experiences can of course be done using quantitative methods. This is not the conclusion that Aigen reaches, however. He links clinical experience to qualitative research, giving the impression that he wants to elevate the prestige of clinicians by calling their work research. Clinicians normally do not quantify their data. If I want to define what they are doing as being research, this is possible only when quantitative research as such is considered less essential. This obscures the difference between clinical work and research. I agree that the fact that clinicians do not quantify their data cannot on its own be an obstacle to calling them researchers; however, this does not change the previous conclusion that clinical work can be called research only when these clinical experiences are analyzed, when we know how this analysis has taken place, and if other researchers can repeat this analysis. A strong point in Aigen's argument is that the clinic is the laboratory and that no experimental procedure ever can elucidate the naturalistic treatment situation. When he writes, however, that he hopes to raise the status of music therapy practice by demonstrating that most of it is grounded in research, albeit research without such traditional validation tools as experimentally designed outcome studies, this is a risky point of view. The clinic can be a laboratory only if we apply research techniques that exceed normal clinical practice. Aigen also states that clinical practice is most like qualitative research when it incorporates aspects of "client-centered, humanistic, transpersonal perspectives." From this, we can infer that the humanistic therapist is the best qualitative researcher and that qualitative research methods should be used when humanistic therapy is the focus of research.

That a research method should be open to the essential characteristics of clinical practice is very logical. For instance, studying humanistic therapy without focusing on experiences makes no sense, but I am not sure whether the analogy between qualitative research and humanistic therapy that Aigen suggests holds completely true. To what extent should we equalize the attitudes of the humanistic therapist and the qualitative researcher studying humanistic therapy? Should the qualitative researcher really act as a humanistic therapist? Again, what seems to be missing is the boundary between treatment and research. A qualitative researcher is a researcher who uses qualitative research methods, which must be open to the ongoing experiential processes of therapy, but is the researcher's method the same as the therapist's attitude? For Aigen, both methods are congruent. In his view, qualitative research and music therapy share common ground:

- In qualitative research and humanistic music therapy, the person of researcher and therapist is more important than the techniques he or she uses. The therapist's Self acts as an agent of change, and the researcher's Self is the research instrument. For instance, in both treatment and research, empathy on the part of the therapist/researcher is more important than treatment or research technique.
- In humanistic music therapy, as in qualitative research, individuals are participants and not vehicles with which the therapist/researcher carries out some intervention. Member checking means that there is a negotiation between therapist, researcher, and partici-

pants about process and outcome. This also means that therapist and researcher both are participants themselves and not detached observers.

- Humanistic music therapists and qualitative researchers alike use a trusting and secure human relationship to receive honest, in-depth, personal information from participants. In research, only this type of relationship leads to credible outcomes.

- Humanistic music therapists and qualitative researchers both make use of their personal reactions to the field of study and the clients.

- Qualitative research and humanistic music therapy both value the unique and individual. Qualitative researchers study an individual in the natural context, while the humanistic music therapist seeks to develop the client's individuality. Both qualitative researchers and music therapists prefer the case-study report.

- The peer debriefing used by qualitative researchers and the *supervision* used by music therapists are alike. In peer debriefing, researchers' biases are probed, providing an opportunity for catharsis. Supervision supports the therapist by reflecting the personal and methodological aspects of the treatment process.

- In qualitative research, there is not a fixed method, there is no recipe, and the method reflects the individual characteristics of the researcher. The researcher is flexible and creative. In music therapy, the music therapist is a creative improviser. Neither treatment nor research is directive.

- The qualitative researcher represents multiple constructions of reality. Music therapists try to understand the client's experience and to stimulate clients within a group to share multiple perspectives; they do not give "right" answers or "correct" interpretations.

Although I support Aigen's general line of reasoning, I would like to make some comments. Using their own human resources is an important tool to help qualitative researchers understand and feel what is going on. When doing this, they take the attitude of therapists, empathizing just as therapists do; however, as researchers, they should do more than this. I believe it is not enough for researchers to write down their own empathic experiences. To research means to collect, integrate, and methodically reflect on intrasubjective and intersubjective experiences. Researchers take a metaview, not just writing down their own views.

The second statement confirms the equality of status between researcher and participants, a system in which all can negotiate. In today's health-care system, the client is seen as an autonomous customer able to take part in this negotiation. When we conduct research, however, I think it is important that we draw the line at the therapist or client taking the role of research participant. Interaction between researcher and therapist should be fully equal; therefore, being a member of a research team is different from a training situation or traditional quantitative research, in which one person—the teacher or the researcher—may act as a superior. Equality implies that the researcher's and therapist's roles are equal and that they both give each other complete access to all personal thoughts, intuitions, feelings, and insecurities. If the client were to have equal access to these data, he or she might find some of them upsetting. Also, there is the problem that to some extent, therapist and researcher plan interventions that will have no effect if they have to be corroborated by the client first. The same holds for the assessment. It is unwarranted to give a client access to information when he or she is not yet able to understand or contain it. We should not forget that member checking was originated with work done by Yvonna Lincoln and Egon Guba, who developed research approaches outside therapy situations. In therapy, member checking might cause problems when it confuses the client's progress, when unconscious processes come into play, or when because of client handicaps there is no equality on a cognitive level. Is it realistic, then, to suppose that there always can be complete equality between therapist and client or between researcher and client?

When I read the third statement, I want to ask whether the researcher must adopt a therapeutic human relationship with the client to get credible data. Of course, it is important that the researcher be trustworthy and that the ethical code is met by obtaining informed consent, but if there is both researcher and therapist, the researcher should not enter into the same relationship with the client as the therapist does. When the therapist is the researcher, it is difficult to differentiate between the therapeutic human relationship and the researcher's role (see Ken Bruscia's stance on the issue of authenticity, discussed in Chapter 9).

Every therapist, not just the humanistic therapist, focuses on the individual client because helping the individual client is the main aim of all therapies. Here, Aigen identifies individuality with self-actualization, thus identifying the focus of qualitative research with that of self-actualization therapy. Qualitative research can be used to study other therapeutic schools in which self-actualization plays a less important role, however. Aigen's effort to closely link qualitative research to humanistic, creative, self-actualizing therapy is somehow reductionistic; we have seen in examples described in this book that qualitative research is not solely humanistically oriented.

Although Aigen declares the case study to be common ground between qualitative research and therapy, it is important to remember that there is a difference between traditional case studies and those used in qualitative research. The latter develop through qualitative intra- and intersubjective techniques, whereas the former are therapists' personal views of the story of treatment.

The sixth statement draws parallels between peer debriefing and supervision. I have already have said that doing research is different from being in training. I would like to add that peer debriefing and supervision are different, too. There is personal supervision, in which music therapists receive personal guidance, which should not be part of the peer debriefing process in research. Peer debriefing should concentrate on colleague corroboration of research findings. At first glance, this may seem like work supervision during training or work intersupervision by colleagues, both of which concentrate on the treatment process and not on the therapist as a person, but it is more than that. In work supervision, there is no equality between participants. In work intersupervision, there is equality, but the research techniques of collecting, integrating, and reflecting on data are not used.

The analogy (in the seventh statement) between qualitative researcher and music therapist as flexible, creative actors is metaphorical. Perhaps they *are* both improvisers, but improvisation during the research process differs from musical improvisation. I have another more fundamental objection to this analogy: music therapists and qualitative researchers do not always act as creative improvisers. Music therapists often highly structure sessions, starting with a greeting song, singing an already well known song, asking the client to complete sentences in new songs, and finishing with a good-bye song. Qualitative researchers do not always improvise, instead making use of well-known research methods.

In another paper (1996a), Aigen discusses the problem of values, saying that the qualitative paradigm demands its own sets of values for evaluating research. One of the values he discusses is the researcher's personal context. In qualitative research, it is important to include the researcher's value system. In Aigen's terms, a qualitative researcher should be explicit about his or her motivation for conducting the study, prior experiences, group memberships, and the nature of the relationship between investigator and participants. To be honest, when I first read these points, I thought they were not really important. They conjured up memories linked to what has been called the "battle of positivism" of the 1960s, when "value-free," dialectical philosophers and sociologists discussed "value-free" science. I thought Aigen's points were relevant only in a social-interest context, but then several experiences changed my mind.

For instance, regarding when working with participants, we must make explicit the relationships between roles. If there is not equality between therapist and researcher, we never know what the therapist really thinks. If there is no feedback from the client at all, we never know if research findings really reflect the client's experiences. I remember a qualitative single-case research project in which the client forced herself to be helpful because she thought I was doing the research for my doctoral degree (which was not the case). This client, who had accommodated others all her life, hesitated to react when she did not agree with some of my research hypotheses. Although several times I emphasized that the research was being conducted only for her sake, it became clear to me only after some time that she felt that the research findings did not reflect her experiences. Maybe my behavior as a researcher for her was a sign that I wanted to be perceived as successful, so she forced herself to not disturb my success. This realization made me self-critical and I reflected on such issues as why I was doing this research; whether it was for the client's sake, for my profession, or for my own prestige; and whether I was trying to verify my own theoretical ideas. Because in qualitative research the researcher is the instrument, these personal considerations are more important than in quantitative research, in which the person of the researcher plays a less important role. In qualitative research, the researcher can be the instrument only when his or her value system is reflected upon.

In the same paper, Aigen discusses ethical and methodological concerns when researchers study their own clinical work. Two fundamental questions are important here: Should research be conducted while therapy is in progress? Should the therapist serve as the researcher? Aigen does not differentiate between the two questions, mentioning four possible objections that others have raised against the therapist's conducting research while therapy is in progress:

- The researcher looks for only those outcomes that strengthen music therapists' prestige.
- The research agenda affects the therapist's clinical choices.
- The client unconsciously wants to be a "good" research subject.
- The research process changes the therapist's interventions.

Aigen disagrees with all four objections, concluding that any such conflicts can be managed and that studying the treatment can benefit the client. I completely agree with him that research can be done during treatment because the client may benefit from it. The fourth objection does not stand up because the aim of research is to improve the effectiveness of—and thus change—the therapist's interventions.

Unlike Aigen, however, I want to address the fundamental question of clinicians as researchers. I feel that rejecting the first objection about prestige might be a fruitful rationalization for some therapist-researchers. In discussions with music therapists from different schools of music therapy, I have often experienced fear when I said to them, "If I am going to participate in this study, I want to make sure that I am allowed to write down everything that comes to mind." Some of these music therapists have then decided not to continue with a particular study. I understand their position personally, because being critical of yourself is possible at many institutions only if your position there is already strong. In terms of research, however, this argument is very weak, so I must disagree with Aigen. The first objection he raises is really one against combining the role of therapist and researcher. I favor conducting research with more than one person—not to make it more "objective" but to be sure to indeed allow multiple perspectives to develop.

The second and third objections—and the fourth—are not really objections against the therapist as researcher but against doing research while treatment is in progress. That clinical choices should not be affected by the research agenda holds for quantitative research but not for qualitative, which is naturalistic. The effects on research of the client who unconsciously wants to be a "good" research subject, as in the example above, are managed in quantitative research by the use of "double-blind" studies. This solution is, of course, impossible in qualitative research because the human relationship is so important to that paradigm. It is this same human relationship, however, that can prevent the client from playing the role of "good" subject. We can conclude from this that three of the objections Aigen quotes are not against the therapist's serving as researcher. By rejecting these objections, then, we have not validated the concept of clinician as researcher.

USING CONSTRUCTS

Aigen conducted a qualitative study during a year spent with a group of developmentally delayed adolescents (1995a). The researcher videotaped the sessions, made notes directly after the sessions, and interviewed the two Nordoff-Robbins therapists. He defines this research as naturalistic, using Lincoln and Guba's definition (1985) of studying events in their natural context and searching for patterns. Naturalistic research differs from phenomenological research because there is neither a search for deeper meanings that are not directly expressed in the data nor the interpretations that we would expect in hermeneutic studies (Aigen, 1995b). Its aim is to discover regularities in the data. Grounded theory also searches for regularities (categories and their connections), but it focuses on theory, while naturalistic inquiry does not. As in other types of qualitative research, data are segmented and categorized (coded). Aigen describes the dialectical process between segmenting and categorizing: each category is tentative and changes when subsequent observations are made.

To give you a better understanding of the specific characteristics of the qualitative method Aigen uses, I will describe several of its aspects. Typical of his method is the use of constructs, borrowed from Garner (1986) and defined by Aigen as statements the researcher writes in the first person, as if a study participant, inferring the participant's thoughts, feelings, and actions (Aigen, 1995c; see Ely et al., 1995). In "Here We Are in Music: One Year with An Adolescent Creative Music Therapy Group," a monologue has been written for each of four clients. A strong argument for this is that the clients are described as individuals. The reason for using constructs is that the clients cannot speak for themselves. From this, we can clearly see that Aigen sees a qualitative researcher as acting like a therapist who empathically tries to understand the client's thoughts and feelings. I will illustrate one of Aigen's constructs with excerpts from the monologues and then comment. In the first excerpt, the researcher (Aigen) writes from the perspective of Joey, one of the clients:

> Alan [the therapist] plays a lot of songs just for me. There is "Happy Feet" and "Oh, Rats!" I love to dance around in circles when Alan plays. It makes me very happy. He's funny. Sometimes when I want the furry drum or my other favorite song, "Friends in Music" and I can't get it, I get mad and say, "Oh, rats!" Alan plays and sings, "Oh, rats! You have to wait your turn today." Then I get up and dance and sometimes I forget why I was angry. I'll tell you a secret: sometimes I pretend I'm angry just so Alan will play "Oh, Rats!" and I can get to dance! (Aigen, 1995a)

Some of these interpretations can be made because of what has been observed in, for instance, quotations and actions from the group members. When Joey dances while Alan plays, then the researcher can suppose that Joey feels happy. This does not imply, however, that, as the constructs suggest, Joey reflects on his own state, saying to himself, "I love to dance" and "It makes me happy." Other interpretations, such as "I forget why I was angry" and "I'll tell you a secret" are even more hypothetical. What I am saying is that the researcher, when writing down these constructs, should make clear how these interpretations are grounded in the data. I would advocate working with a research team, developing these constructs dialectically through interaction between coresearchers.

Aigen also interviewed both therapists. In the transcripts, we read how the music therapists reflected their own feelings:

> We [the therapists] hated it! Every time they requested that song ["Old McDonald"], we hated it! It was as if they were pretending "We don't know how to sing that anymore." And it really threw us off. They were still acting like "All right, well, I'm just a little kid still, and let's play this little-kid song and let's all be happy together." [Meanwhile,] they're throwing things, they're pinching, they're stepping on each other's feet, they're yelling at each other" (Aigen, 1995a).

We can also read why the music therapists chose a directive approach:

> (Music therapist:) I've really seen how you need to be more directive and active in bringing [more regressed individuals] out of something, giving them an experience that they would not normally bring themselves to . . .

and why they later on relinquished control to the group members. Making the musical therapists' process of "clinical reasoning" overt is very important; it helps us understand why the music therapists act as they do.

Further, the research report authentically reflects Aigen's own conflict in studying therapy while also, as a clinician, disagreeing with the directive interventions the music therapists chose. In my opinion, this conflict should not only be described but also methodologized in a dialectical interactive process between therapist and researcher. This can be of great benefit for the client because the researcher forces the music therapist to reflect on his or her choices and because it can improve theorizing. It is a strong argument in favor of doing research during treatment.

The researcher taped the sessions himself and thus was selecting the data (not in the therapy room, but sitting in another room from which he could handle the camera). In my view, Aigen, by saying that all scientists create their data and choose their theories, too easily bypasses the fact that his perspective decided "what was going on." In his approach, the researcher's role in selecting data is dominant from the very start. I believe, however, that there are other possible ways to select data. Although Aigen used member checking—the therapists read the monograph written by the researcher—there was not a complete database in which he could ground his interpretations. There are only selected fragments of the process that depended on choices made intuitively by the researcher behind the camera or that were remembered by the music therapists as a result of selective attention while engaged in therapy. I favor having independent coresearchers, who sit behind the one-way screen or view a videotape not preselected by the researcher, describe the session.

Because of the researcher's role, this method comes close to being more action oriented. What I mean is that, as Aigen himself points out, the researcher becomes a participant in the group process. By selecting data, he or she influences the therapist's perception and thus becomes part of the process, not just describing but also influencing what is going on. By saying that he selects only those incidents that support his interpretation, Aigen stresses that the quality of data, not its quantity, is important. Nevertheless, this resembles the process of naive verification, instead of continuously trying to develop different patterns of understanding. The researcher's perspective seems to be very dominant.

What is important in Aigen's research method, as in the Nordoff-Robbins approach, is the principle that a research report should include descriptions of the music. Aigen says this is necessary because participants' experiences are contained in the music (Aigen, 1996a). It is indeed important to explore not only the story behind the tones but also the connection between the musical process and the story behind it. We must understand how the psychological processes are resounded in the musical processes. Although using songs with self-created words give insight into psychological processes, the musical characteristics of the songs express emotional processes. How clients express themselves and interact in purely musical processes is unclear.

Aigen presents three significant research findings: (1) the connection between physical actions and the music, (2) the functions served by the music (easing transition points in therapy, meeting group and individual needs, stimulating emotional and interactional experiences), and (3) the relevance of group process theory (power struggles, the reaching of deeper levels of contact, relationships between members).

The first finding is clearly an example of the Nordoff-Robbins music therapy philosophy, in which—as is the case with one client, Edward—changing disruptive behavior into musical behavior is seen as the main purpose of music therapy. This finding is not really new, and because both therapists in this study were Nordoff-Robbins therapists, it is somehow self-evident. What is interesting in terms of research is the therapists' and researcher's quest for meaning behind one client's (Andrew's) throwing instruments and falling. After the therapists gave a meaning to the behavior ("throwing instruments and falling means avoiding musical contact"), this interpretation directed their intervention and finally changed the disruptive behavior into musically meaningful actions. The research process did indeed influence therapy. Let me summarize how meaning became grounded in the data. Aigen writes:

> Throughout the year, I wondered about the significance of throwing and falling. The possibilities included that they were aggressive acts, actions to gain attention or elicit reprimands, actions geared toward limiting his musical involvement, or possibly . . . his way of saying that musical contact was too painful or difficult and this was his only way of limiting such contact (Aigen, 1995a).

The last hypothesis was conceptualized as an inner conflict ("conflicting feelings about contact") and was grounded as follows:

- Andrew engages in actions that remove him from the group, but he also wants to return to the circle.
- Sometimes he comes close to falling but then stops himself.
- At the end of the session, his need for distance increases: he takes an instrument he can throw, and because of this, he will be removed from the group.

The change in this inner conflict when therapy progressed was also grounded by events:

- Andrew spins the tambourine on one finger, but does not drop it.
- He drops the drum very gently to the floor and in time with the cymbal crash.
- He feigns throwing one of the sticks but holds on to it.
- He throws the stick with one hand and catches it with the other.

Aigen, reflecting after these events on the therapists' clinical reasoning process, writes that "both therapists decided that this throwing represented efforts to avoid contact and they decided not to support this avoidance by so quickly ending his opportunities to play."

Besides making "physical statements," Aigen describes developments in physical contact. Where a quantitative researcher would use an observation scale, Aigen looks at dimensions of physical contact, such as desired/undesired, sanctioned/proscribed, between group members or group members/therapists, antecedents/consequences of contact, affectionate versus aggressive, and finally, social value according to context. Here, we recognize the search for patterns that is part of naturalistic research. The researcher's description of patterns is corroborated by the music therapists' session reports.

It is interesting to read how physical contact reflects group interactions: Diana puts her arms around Joey, and they both look at Andrew as Joey says, "Don't you dare touch her!" What is missing from this aspect of the process, however, is a description of the music therapy. This is a typical group process, but it does not give us any information about music therapy. At times, the definitions of the music's functions does not lead to new statements. Aigen writes, for instance: "Music was also used to both contain and transform physical actions or expressions" and "Music was also used to compensate for language deficits." The therapists' techniques, such as matching the physical movements to communicate acceptance, fulfilling individual and group needs by taking turns in a group activity, are not really new.

Other functions add something new, especially by the way they are described. For instance, the way transition points are described musically is very illustrative: Diana, when introduced to the group, immediately took part by playing the drum, becoming a successful part of the group. Also, one description of the way the therapist succeeded in fulfilling both individual group needs gives strong support for the benefits of music therapy: the therapist accompanied the movements of Joey, who disrupted the group, while still staying in the tonality of the group's song. Although using the concept of effect would not be appropriate when discussing naturalistic research along the lines of Lincoln and Guba's methods, sentences such as "Music functioned to extend and deepen the duration and quality of the contact" sound to me as if music had an effect upon the duration and quality of contact. When Aigen describes how the music therapists reflect upon ". . . isolating the factors that mediated this change in the group process," he refers to Lincoln and Guba's concept of mutual simultaneous shaping, which I believe comes close to being the circular causality of systemic therapy.

The way Aigen writes his research report differs from traditional standards. For instance, the methodological considerations have been put into an appendix, not at the beginning of the report. It also is not just a longitudinal description: the same interactions are referred to more than once because they have significance for several areas of discussion.

Let us discuss Aigen's values as a researcher (1996a):

- The research should have relevance for the therapists
- The research should include multiple perspectives, from all the individuals involved.
- The narrative form of reporting should reflect the content, not merely the procedures.
- Understanding processes in music therapy requires contextualizing them—getting a feel for the research participants as individuals.

A lot of qualitative researchers see the first point as the strongest argument against research that has no immediate practical significance. I object: does research always need to be practical? There is no doubt that research of benefit for music therapy practice is important, but research of benefit in external communication—in forums of professionals and researchers outside music therapy—is also needed. Why should we be prohibited from using types of research appropriate for these forums, as long as we keep in mind that the research does not reflect the particular music therapy because it has another purpose? Although quantitative effect research is reductionistic and of limited clinical significance, it can produce needed findings. This is not merely a political argument; I believe that many other practitioners also long for evidence that music therapy has a statistically significant effect, evidence they can use to strengthen not only their professional status but also their self-confidence. I think there should be not an either-or research paradigm but an eclectic or integrative one.

The second point (regarding multiple perspectives) brings up a problem in using constructs. I understand that Aigen wants to explain clients' perspectives because they cannot do so themselves, but he does so by drawing on his own empathy. Is it correct to say, then, that these are their perspectives? Are they not the therapist-researcher's perspective on their perspective? When the researcher uses constructs, there are no multiple perspectives but only one researcher who develops all perspectives. Of course, this is normal in treatment, in which clients cannot verbalize in psychological terminology, but should it be transferred to research?

As we have discussed throughout this book, There is an ongoing discussion about the criteria for appropriateness of qualitative studies. In this debate Aigen subscribes to the arguments made by Lincoln and Guba (1985) that in qualitative research, criteria are needed, such as credibility, transferability, dependability, and confirmability. I believe, as I have said several times, that too often, researchers identify such traditional concepts as internal validity, external validity, and reliability with quantitative research techniques rather than deal with the basic questions behind them that can be applied to qualitative research. I prefer the traditional criteria not because I believe they can ever be used in the same way in qualitative research but because I believe they focus on basic facets of human insight and can facilitate communication between quantitative and qualitative researchers.

Chapter 11

RESEARCHERS AS COACTORS*

INTRODUCTION

The research method I developed is an example of action research because the research enhances treatment outcome. Treatment is in no way disturbed by research artificialities, but the research influences treatment by means of feedback from the researcher's analyses and discussions among members of the research team. My method can be described as *naturalistic* inquiry (Lincoln and Guba, 1985), although it differs in some respects (see discussions of trustworthiness in previous chapters in this book). A primary principle of this type of research method is its flexibility: for each case, I use all available and necessary techniques.

I will illustrate this type of research by describing, in retrospect, some portions of the short-term treatment (24 sessions) of a little girl of 7, Helen, and her mother, described in more detail in "Becoming Friends with Your Mother: Techniques of Qualitative Research Illustrated with Examples from the Short-Term Treatment of a Girl Who Wetted Herself"(Smeijsters and Storm, in press). I will first describe the members of the research team, then give a short overview of the research tools used.

*Portions of this chapter are modified from Smeijsters and Storm (1997), with permission. I developed this research method during my affiliation with the Music Therapy Laboratory at the Hogeschool van Arnhem in Nijmegen, The Netherlands (1989–1996). Presently, I am establishing the Creative Arts Therapy Advanced Research Centre (CATARC) at the Hogeschool Limburg in Sittard, The Netherlands.

THE RESEARCH METHOD

The Research Team

The research team for this case was made up of three people: the music therapist, the researcher, and an observer. After each session, the music therapist wrote a self-report and the researcher wrote an observation report about the audiovisual tape; during therapy, the observer wrote an observation report from behind the one-way screen. (In other cases, clients themselves also make a self-report.) All reports were written independently, without any guidelines, because they were meant to describe experiences as openly as possible. The music therapist's descriptions often contained his objectives, observations, and personal feelings about progress in music therapy. The observer behind the one-way screen gave her impressions of what was happening, without knowing the music therapist's intentions, and the researcher, through repeatedly observing the audiovisual tape, made a detailed reconstruction of all verbal, nonverbal, and musical behavior during the session. In all reports, cognitive arguments, emotional experiences, and musical analyses were part of the description.

The Transcript and Member Checking

After each session, the researcher made a transcript of the self-reports written by the music therapist and the observer and of the observation report he himself had written when reviewing the audiovisual tape. Transcripts of sessions were handed over to the music therapist, the observer, and the mother for member checking: checking the data, themes, interpretations, and conclusions with the very people under study (Lincoln and Guba, 1985; Ely et al., 1995). The music therapist discussed the transcripts with the mother during home visits. It is the music therapist's task to (1) discuss with the team whether and at what points member checking can contribute to the therapy process and (2) introduce and discuss it with the client during the session. It is my experience that member checking, when it is introduced properly, can contribute to the client's personal process, depending on the client's condition. In some cases, the client may feel confronted, disturbed, or confused by team members' reports and member checking can disturb the therapeutic relationship. In Helen and her mother's case, member checking gave the mother insight and helped her to reflect on her own way of communicating. Discussing the transcript during the session was impossible because Helen was present; therefore, the music therapist made home calls and visits.

Circular iterative feedback by analytical memos (see below) and live team discussions between researcher, music therapist, and observer were also part of member checking. During intrateam member checking, the music therapist, observer, and researcher establish a dialectical interaction in which they played devil's advocate for one another. The group was not searching for some sort of "truth," defined as those data upon which everybody agrees, because doing so would have led to experiential reductionism. With this process, the researcher respects multiple perspectives and uses them to corroborate, adjust, or make more complete his or her own interpretations. Member checking also provides an opportunity for catharsis.

Peer Debriefing

The psychotherapist and family therapist from the psychotherapeutic outpatient treatment institution where Helen and her mother were in treatment also at times received a copy of the complete research report and were asked to comment on it. They acted as experts not involved with the treatment provided by the music therapist. Their role could therefore be described as an example of peer debriefing or peer checking: checking for biases and testing working hypotheses by asking independent experts to interpret the data themselves (Lincoln and Guba 1985; Ely et al., 1995). During interviews with the music therapist, they were invited to challenge the research team's hypotheses. The music therapist wrote reports of these conversations that were integrated into the transcripts.

Categories, Analytical Memos, Circular Iterative Feedback, and Repeated Analysis

While making a transcript of each report, the researcher marked those words he thought could be of importance. He accomplished this with the aid of categories, a classification of concepts developed by comparing concepts against others and grouping them together because they appear to pertain a similar phenomenon (Strauss and Corbin, 1990). After each session, he wrote several analytical memos (Ely et al., 1995), in which he combined marked words to comprise diagnostic themes; discussed the music therapist's objectives, play forms, and techniques; and reflected on the link between diagnosis and treatment and on the music therapist's therapeutic attitude. He also used analytical memos to interpret the clients' experiences during musical play and to propose alternative suggestions on how to proceed to the music therapist. The music therapist and observer gave feedback on these analytical memos and thus checked the researcher's data processing, categories, themes, interpretations, and conclusions. This feedback process was circular and was repeated many times, which is known as circular iterative feedback. *Repeated analysis* refers to the researcher's regularly comparing old data with new and thus checking his previous hypotheses. The researcher checked whether the old data corroborated his latest interpretations, whether previous interpretations needed to be changed, or whether previous interpretations could be used for old data. New data, however, require new interpretations.

Diagnostic Themes

After several sessions, the researcher developed diagnostic themes by combining similar marked diagnostic words, the diagnostic hypotheses from the analytical memos, and some categories. A theme is a statement of meaning that runs through all or most of the pertinent data by linking data in and across categories (Ely et al., 1995). These diagnostic themes have been called focus points. By means of member checking with the music therapist and the observer, the team can develop treatment goals, play forms, and techniques and describe and analyze treatment progress.

Triangulation

Triangulation involves the use of different personal sources (the mother, the music therapist, the observer, the researcher, the psychotherapist, and the family therapist), the use of different data-collecting techniques (self-reports, observation reports, interviews, discussions), and the exploration of several theoretical models of treatment (Lincoln and Guba, 1985; Ely et al., 1995).

The Chain of Evidence

All data, categories, themes, interpretations, and conclusions are registered in the research report, making it possible for a second independent researcher to replicate the chain of evidence, meaning to investigate the links between the data collected and the conclusions drawn (Yin, 1989).

EXAMPLES AND COMMENTS

Analytical Memos

An analytical memo from session 15 reads as follows:

Memo 5 (after Session 15)
Mother is not able to respond musically to the child. She seems exhausted, does not react to the child's initiative, and seems to have lost influence. Perhaps if she could react playfully to the child, her influence could be restored. When she gives parental directives, the child does not obey or accept her leading role.

After session 16, this same memo was extended as follows:

Memo 5 (from Session 15,
Revised after Session 16)

Mother is unable verbally and nonverbally to show empathy when the child cries. If she would be more active at times when the child needs emotional support, she could restore a little bit of the influence she is longing for. Instead of being empathic, she only gives directives and by this claims power the child is not willing to accept. The music therapist can advise the mother to try:

1. To be more playful during musical improvisation
2. Not to withdraw musically but gain some musical personality—being there
3. To reduce the frequency of directives and support the child by verbal and musical empathy

Until now, there has been a battle of power that the mother is unable to win. Only by bypassing this battle will changes be possible.

Whereas the transcripts of the reports contain only superficial interpretations, analytical memos give interpretations and conclusions on a deeper level. Because they are tentative, will often be changed, and may be of less importance when therapy proceeds, analytical memos are excluded from member checking with clients during therapy.

Live Member Checking within the Team

One of the live member checks within the team had been scheduled when the music therapist felt insecure about progress. In the research report, this was summarized as follows:

Member Checking (after Session 23)

Because the music therapist felt insecure about progress, a special member-checking meeting was held. The researcher and observer asked the music therapist to explore his feelings. The music therapist expressed disappointment because Helen had started wetting herself again, because it was difficult to let Helen's younger sister Edith share the musical play, because the musical interplay was difficult to direct, and because the mother had little chance to express herself musically.

The music therapist forgot what, in the researcher and observer's view, had been gained by this time: a significant improvement of the relationship between Helen and her mother. The music therapist probably became a bit confused because of the frequent presence of little Edith, which gradually changed the course of music therapy. Now that the focus of therapy changed to Edith, the dynamics of the whole family came into view and cooperation had to be extended to three people.

Exploring the music therapist's feelings is part of qualitative research. The perspectives of the other research team members can help him or her to reframe and stimulate him or her to develop new ideas for treatment. Although this resembles supervision, it is not the same because the research techniques and focus are meant to fulfill the criterion of a self-monitored, systematic gathering of data relevant to a community of researchers (Bruscia, 1996a)

DIAGNOSTIC THEMES (FOCUS POINTS) AND TREATMENT

In the first phase of treatment one of the focus points was labeled "insecurity":

Insecurity (Sessions 6 through 16)
The child was referred to music therapy because she wet her clothes at school. The mother, when interviewed by the music therapist, told him that she thought the child was insecure. During therapy, when the music therapist explains a play form to Helen, she often reacts by saying, "I don't understand." She stops musical play and changes musical activity quickly. At other times, she lies down on top of the drum, slaps the piano with her hands, or grasps sticks from her

mother. There is little musical development, variation, or initiative in Helen's play. Often, she imitates the music therapist's or her mother's initiatives.

Treatment goals that developed as a result of the therapist's suggestions and the researcher's treatment hypotheses, developed in memos and during member checks within the team were experiencing joy, prolonging musical play, stimulating initiative, and stimulating creativity. Integration of marked words in the transcript of the events during musical play showed the development of a close relationship between music therapist and client and of creativity in Helen's musical play. Helen had fun, and although still imitating, she also introduced some musical ideas herself. After some time, this focus point became less important. When treatment proceeded, the transcripts' marked words and the comments in the analytical memos gave rise to another focus point: disturbed relationship with Mother. Although the focus point of security was used as a sensitizing concept (Glaser and Strauss, 1967) that guided the selection of words in forthcoming transcripts, the process of marking transcript words and writing memos was as "open" as possible.

Disturbed Relationship with Mother
(after Session 16)

The child plays very loudly, whereas the mother withdraws. Helen instructs her younger sister Edith how to play the instruments and takes Mother's role. Mother tries to instruct Helen but fails. After her mother's attempts, Helen says, "You make me confused."

There is no musical interplay and little eye contact between Helen and her mother. When Helen cries during the session, telling her mother that because Helen wet her clothes her father had hit her, her mother is unable to react empathically. There seems to be a conflict of power, illustrated by Helen's saying "Oh, no" when she is invited to musically play a boat that is moved by the sea (played by Mother). She also refuses to play, together with Mother, the trees who are moved by the wind (played by the music therapist and Edith). Helen does not want to exchange chairs with Mother and keeps Mother from playing by grasping her sticks.

This focus point resulted from previous sessions' data and became the central focus of sessions 17 through 23. If we compare this focus point with the earlier one of "insecurity," then it is obvious that Helen's grasping the sticks began to be interpreted differently. By integrating the first and second focus point with additional information from the intake interview, the research team developed the following local diagnostic theory:

Local Diagnostic Theory

In the interview, the mother had said that she as a child never experienced affection herself. She was raised by her grandmother, who did not accept her affectively. Because she did not experience affection herself, perhaps she is unable to give it. This led to Helen's lacking basic trust in her mother and becoming insecure. Helen's insecurity increased after a second child (Edith) had been born and when Helen had to attend school.

Helen overcompensated for this insecurity by trying to take over Mother's parental role, thus crossing generation boundaries, and by not following her directions, fighting with her about power, and forcing her to withdraw.

The interaction between Helen and her mother became circular because when Mother withdrew, Helen gained more influence, which resulted in Mother's withdrawing even more.

This local diagnostic theory was meant to organize all the different parts of information into a credible picture. The research team members worked together to develop the following treatment goals: restoring the relationship, strengthening the mother's role, and repairing generation boundaries.

Triangulation

Because diagnosis and goals had shifted from an individual to a relational focus, the researcher decided to explore family-therapy theories that might be of help in describing interactions. He began a study of the literature and came up with several theoretical perspectives, such as systemic family therapy (Murray Bowen), strategic family therapy (Jay Haley), and structural family therapy (Salvador Minuchin). Because structural family therapy focuses on conflicts, hierarchy, alliances, coalitions, and generation boundaries, the research team concluded that this model could contribute most to understanding Helen's relationship with her mother. The team used concepts from structural family therapy to code the data. The musical play forms were called "enactments," arranged by the music therapist as stage manager, showing spontaneous behaviors that reflected the family process—for instance, the child saying "Oh, no!" when she was invited to musically play the boat that was moved by the sea, played by her mother. Structural family therapy also suggested the "theory" that the mother had adopted to explain her daughter's behavior ("trying to get attention"). There was "circularity" because the mother's withdrawal increased Helen's dominant behavior and because of the problems concerning "hierarchy" and conflict of power. The boundaries between generations had faded because Helen constantly instructed Edith.

OUTCOMES

Musical Play Forms

With the help of the concepts of alliance and coalition, the team developed musical play forms to reach therapeutic goals. In structural family therapy, an alliance is cooperation among people so that they can complete a task together. A coalition is cooperation to "fight the enemy." I will give several examples of alliances and coalitions introduced by the music therapist.

Alliances
Singing together became a regular part of therapy. These songs were accompanied by instruments. When they sang a song called "Toddle Men," the music therapist played the song on his guitar, Helen played on a wooden drum, and the mother played a split drum. The child played the song's meter and the mother played its rhythm. In the "Crocodile Song," mother and child played the same rhythm together.

They were able to do the same thing musically without quarreling and fighting.

Coalitions

The first coalition occurred when the music therapist instructed Helen and her mother to sing "Toddle Men" together while he was attempting to sing in canon. Helen and mother formed a musical coalition against the music therapist, who failed to sing the canon correctly, leading to a relaxed atmosphere between Mother and Helen.

Sometimes later, the music therapist introduced a musical play, in which the therapist starts with a rhythmic motif that is to be answered by a rhythmic three-tone motif played by the client, called the "boom-boom-boom play." The music therapist verbally introduced the play by telling Helen and her mother that they should play the three-tone motif together.

This play sounds like a musical exercise, but in essence, it brought the mother and child together. Because the music therapist made a lot of variations, the play was very funny and there was a lot of laughter. He tried to confuse mother and child, who had to be very attentive to each other to counteract his tricks. They could succeed and oppose his challenges only when they formed a coalition. As a result, the mother and child looked and listened carefully to each other, the mother directed their playing together by her facial expressions, and they succeeded in reacting synchronously in time. Their process of becoming close unfolded in the musical process.

Guidelines

Some of the guidelines developed as an outcome of research in this case were as follows:

- When there is a conflict of power, "leading and following" should be preceded by a parallel activity such as singing, through musical "alliances" and "coalitions." Here, the music therapist acts as the outsider who, by using canons or preludes, tries to synchronize the others.

- Meter and rhythm offer important possibilities for exploring contact at different levels: playing rhythmical variations on a basic meter, playing "off beat," playing a meter or rhythm synchronously.
- The chance to say no can be incorporated into musical play by offering choices of musical instruments, offering alternative sequences of musical play, and giving the client the opportunity to create a pause by hitting a special instrument, such as a gong. Paradoxical intentions can be a helpful procedural technique.
- Generational boundaries can be reestablished when the parents take over the music therapist's role and the children are invited to form a coalition against the parents.
- Children who are frequently overruled by their parents can be invited to take a leading role or play a prestigious instrument.

In this case, changes in family-therapy treatment at the outpatient institution took away the parents' motivation to continue family and music therapy.

Arguments about Music's Role

Arguments about music's role are based on a type of musical analysis that differs from traditional musical analysis because it involves a search for analogies between musical syntax, musical semantics, and personal aspects. I suppose that in musical expressions and interactions, specific and nonspecific analogies of psychic and social processes can be heard (Smeijsters, 1993, 1996a). The following arguments give support to the hypothesis that these analogies occurred in this particular treatment and that they were important agents of therapeutic development:

- The mother illustrated her weak position by playing pitchlessly and softly. The child expressed resistance by playing very loudly and dynamically interfering with her mother's playing. These musical behaviors are called specific analogies because the behaviors are expressed in musical parameters (pitch, dynamics).

- The child expressed rebelliousness in a nonspecific way by grasping her mother's sticks. This is nonspecific behavior because it can happen during lots of activities and is not characterized by specific expressions in musical parameters.
- Musical improvisations, musical plays, and singing turned out to be analogies of improved communication processes. Because singing together is not an exchange but doing the same thing together, it is an easy way of cooperating. Nevertheless, there is cooperation because singing together requires exact timing and intonation, forcing one to pay attention to the other singers. The canon and the "boom-boom-boom play" that the therapist used turned out to be a successful means to make Helen and mother form a coalition against the music therapist.
- The mother, when discussing the research report with the music therapist, immediately recognized similarities between musical interaction and interaction processes at home. By saying "In music therapy, it is less heavy, more playful," not only did she corroborate the analogy between music therapy and interaction processes at home, but she also felt that in music therapy, there was some progress in the behaviors exhibited in normal life.

SUMMARY

The table below summarizes the main research concepts and techniques I use.

Research Techniques and Outcomes	Descriptions and Comments
Transcripts	Transcripts are made of all self-reports (by client and music therapist), observations (observer and researcher)
Analytical memos	In these, the researcher combines marked words to form diagnostic themes; discusses the music therapist's objectives, play forms, and techniques; and reflects on the link between diagnosis and treatment and on the music therapist's therapeutic attitude. Analytical memos are also used to interpret the client's personal experiences during musical play and to propose alternative suggestions on how to proceed to the music therapist.
Member checking	Member checking is conducted, for all data, themes, local theories, treatment programs, guidelines, and arguments, within the research team and with the client by means of written feedback, client interviews, and team discussions.
Repeated analysis	The researcher regularly compares old data with new and checks previous hypotheses. The researcher also checks whether old data corroborate the latest interpretations and whether previous interpretations need to be changed or can be used for old data, keeping in mind that new data need new interpretations.
Peer debriefing	Peer debriefing involves searching out biases and testing working hypotheses by asking independent experts to interpret the data.
Categories	Categories are classifications of concepts grouped together because they pertain a similar phenomenon.
Diagnostic themes (focus points)	Diagnostic themes are diagnostic meanings generated from marked words from a couple of sessions and across categories within which essential diagnostic aspects are described and coded.
Local diagnostic theory	A local diagnostic theory is constructed as a result of content analysis of the whole set of sessions.
Treatment proposals	Treatment proposals are suggested indications, goals, objectives, play forms, and techniques of music therapy.

(Continues on next page)

Research Techniques and Outcomes	Descriptions and Comments
Arguments	Arguments are made about progress, possible side effects, disturbances, and catalysts. Side effects are unintended positive or negative effects of treatment. Disturbances are counterproductive factors from outside treatment. Catalysts are outside factors that stimulate treatment.
Triangulation	Triangulation is the use of different personal sources, different data-collecting techniques, and the exploration of several theoretical models.
Results	
Play forms and guidelines	Guidelines are rules of thumb that may be used in similar cases.
Arguments about music's role	These arguments give support to the hypothesis that analogies occurred in treatment that were important agents of therapeutic development.
Replication of the chain of evidence	An independent researcher attempts to replicate the researcher's process of reasoning based on the data.

Chapter 12

MISCELLANEOUS
QUALITATIVE RESEARCH DESIGNS

Categorizing the possibilities of combining the quantitative and qualitative paradigms shows that there are several positions researchers can hold:

- Believing that only qualitative research should be used and that no one researcher can work with both paradigms (for instance, Ken Aigen and Carolyn Kenny)
- Believing that quantitative and qualitative methods should be used in separate research projects (my own position)
- Believing quantitative and qualitative methods can be combined in one research project
- Doubting the scientific benefit of qualitative research

In this chapter, we will discuss several research designs in which quantitative and qualitative techniques were mixed.

A METHOD OF ANALYZING IMPROVISATIONS

General Description

In describing his research method, Lee (1996) begins by saying that although music gives music therapy its unique potential, music itself is difficult to grasp in quantitative as well as qualitative research. I believe that as music therapists, we face at least two problems: the traditional musical analysis musicians use does not say anything about music's personal and therapeutic meaning and on the other hand, the therapeutic concepts borrowed from established schools of psychotherapy are difficult to link to musical processes. Lee introduces a method of analyzing improvisations with which he tries to demystify music from a therapeutic perspective while balancing quantitative and qualitative research methodologies. It is called a method that we can adapt to both research and clinical situations; thus, we must keep in mind Ken Bruscia's cautions differentiating between clinical work and research (discussed in Chapter 9). Here is a short overview of the research stages, which are then explained through a description of Lee's research with clients who have human immunodeficiency virus (HIV) and/or acquired immunodeficiency syndrome (AIDS).

1. **The Therapist Listens Holistically:** The therapist listens several times to the whole improvisation to get a sense of the whole. He or she also tries to identify those musical elements, properties, structures, and processes that reflect the improvisation's fundamental character, taking general notes and listening to the improvisation several times.

2. **The Therapist Reacts to the Music as a Process:** The therapist writes a narrative of how he or she perceives the musical and therapeutic experience. This may include how the improvisation relates to the client's therapy process as well as what the therapist was feeling or thinking during or immediately after the improvisation.

3. **The Client Listens:** The therapist plays the taped improvisation for the client and asks him or her to comment. Each time the client speaks, the therapist stops the music and notes exactly where in the improvisation the client was moved to react.

4. **The Consultant Listens:** The therapist plays the tape for several experts from different professional arenas (musician, verbal psychotherapist, music therapist), noting where in the improvisation the consultants were moved. The therapist tape-records the conversation and makes a complete transcript of it.

5. **The Therapist Notates the Transcript:** The extent of notation depends on the amount of time available and the type technology used. There are many different types of notation.

6. **The Therapist Divides the Improvisation into Musical Components:** The therapist's segmentation of the session into musical sections is guided by specific criteria. The use of sections makes it possible to analyze manageable components in more depth.

7. **The Therapist Compiles a Verbal Description of the Improvisation:** The therapist describes particularly striking, substantial sections of the improvisation as segmented in stage 6. The description must be concise and thus must include only those elements that seem significant.

8. **The Therapist Conducts an In-Depth Analysis of Segments:** At least two segments of the improvisation—those receiving the strongest or most frequent reactions from client and consultants in previous stages—are selected and considered in relation to the entire improvisation. The therapist describes what is the same and what is different between the segments and the whole improvisation. He or she then musically analyzes each segment comprehensively and in depth (theoretical approaches: Heinrich Schenker, Allen Forte, Jean-Jacques Nattiez), focusing on harmonic cells, tonal centers, melodic motifs, characteristic intervals, rhythmic motifs or cells, metric structures, and characteristic textures.

9. **The Therapist Compares Verbal Data against Music Segment Analyses:** The therapist uses the verbal data obtained earlier from clients and consultants in this comparison. This process includes finding agreement and contradiction in the verbal data; linking the verbal remarks to specific musical locations, structures, and elements; explaining what in the music may have accounted for a particular remark; and reconciling contradictions between verbal and musical aspects and between music therapist, client, and consultants.

10. The Therapist Synthesizes All Elements: This step involves integrating all data and drawing conclusions.

From these stages we can see that Lee's method resembles other qualitative research methods that employ holistic listening, repeated analysis by the researcher, subjective self-reports, member checking, and peer debriefing.

In stage 1, we might ask whether focusing on musical elements representing an improvisation's fundamental character produces too restricted a selection. When we compare this stage to, for instance, Bruscia's "Improvisation Assessment Profiles" (1987), in which congruence profiles are used to assess the consistency of the elements of tension level, it is obvious that an element that does not reflect an improvisation's fundamental character can still yield important information.

Stages 2 through 4 belong together and include the feelings, thoughts, images of the music therapist, the client, and the consultants. In stage 2, the music therapist–researcher begins the interpretive process, making use of his or her subjective experience. What is striking here is the fact that the music therapist–researcher seeks to relate the improvisation to the client's therapy process and to note his or her feelings and thoughts during or immediately after the improvisation, whereas in the processes of member checking and peer debriefing, the therapist-researcher aims to select episodes by which the client and consultant were moved. Asking different questions makes it difficult to compare the music therapist's experiences with those of the client and the consultants (see stage 9). In stages 3 and 4, this method supposes that the client's and experts' comments can be closely linked to an episode of music to which the client has just listened. Is it really that easy? Psychic processes during music listening are developing, and feelings, associations, and thoughts may be affected by what has preceded this particular episode. Several qualitative research methods use musical segmenting (see the discussions of morphology in Chapter 6 and of the IMDoS method [Integrative Music Therapy Documentation System] later in this chapter), but it is questionable to what extent fragmenting of music is meaningful. A musical fragment's meaning depends on the total gestalt of which it is part, and musical experience is retrospective and prospective. Is segmenting not equal to positivistic methodology's reduction of experience to variables? Of course, researchers who

want to combine qualitative and quantitative research in one research project will reject this objection because they do not share
the qualitative researcher's paradigm.

Stages 5 through 8 focus on musical analysis. One question
we might ask is why the criteria used to select musical segments
must be established when in stage 8, well-known approaches to
musical analysis are mentioned. Another question is whether this
segmenting should be the task of the individual researcher who
already, in stage 7, identified the "most significant" musical
elements. In stage 8, there are two criteria listed by which segments are selected: those receiving the "strongest" or "most frequent" reactions from the client and consultants. This is a
combination of qualitative and quantitative thinking: selecting
the "strongest" reaction can be defined as a qualitative criterion,
and selecting the "most frequent" reactions, as quantitative. This
brings us to differences between qualitative and quantitative
research: when one person shows a "strong" reaction, qualitative
research accepts this perspective as important even when all
other people involved have no reaction to this particular section.
The problem, however, is how to define *strongest* and *most frequent*. For a quantitative criterion, *most* is vague.

Another important point of discussion in stage 8 is whether
theoretical approaches adopted from Schenker, Forte, or Nattiez
can be of help in describing musical processes in music therapy.
Can their approaches capture the essence of a music therapy
improvisation, or must we develop other musical analyses that
focus from the beginning on the personal and interactional
meaning of musical processes? Lee's method seems to analyze two
different worlds, the personal and the musical, independently and
then compare them to each other.

Analysis of Therapeutic Improvisational Music

In one research project involving clients who had HIV
and/or AIDS, Lee (1995) formulated four hypotheses prior to data
collection:

- It is possible to perceive a direct link between musical
  representation and therapeutic development.

- The musical components of therapeutic improvisation are as important as the therapeutic evaluations in evaluating the efficacy of music therapy.
- Specific musical themes and/or motifs are used to generate therapeutic improvisation as a whole.
- Both client's and therapist's musical preferences and cultures directly affect the musical components incorporated within the therapeutic improvisation.

Lee asked three clients to select one of four piano improvisations from a 1-month session period to represent the stage of the music therapy process. Using a Yamaha musical instrument digital interface (MIDI) grand piano linked to an Apple Macintosh computer, Lee transcribed improvisations and then retranscribed them aurally into normal musical notation with the help of a recording made on a digital audio transport (DAT) tape recorder. He added verbal reflections from the clients and three external validators (a musician, a counselor, and a music therapist). The client listened to his or her own improvisation and was asked to stop the tape and comment when he or she felt something important had happened or there was a general need to say something. The three validators listened to each improvisation and then commented from their professional standpoints.

In stage 1 (stages differ from stages described in the preceding pages), the researcher–music therapist gave an overall picture of the whole therapeutic process. He included reflections from the client during both the therapeutic process and the research session, as well as his own subjective viewpoints and comments from the outside validators. The researcher–music therapist is the one who gives the overall picture and selects comments from the client and validators. There was no member checking and no peer debriefing after the overall view had been composed.

In stage 2, the researcher–music therapist made an overall catalogue of the musical components. The first two stages led to the main investigation: analyzing two sections from the improvisation chosen by the client. The researcher–music therapist made selections on the basis of five criteria: (1) occasions on which there was more than one tape pause (a maximum of four from the client and three validators), (2) periods in which there was an evident density of tape pauses, (3) sections in which the richest amount of material was available, (4) sections that began and ended at points that made grammatical sense, and (5) sections in which the client was included as an active participant in the selection stage.

Next, the researcher–music therapist collected verbal-assessment data. Lee mentions that this stage also incorporated stages 1 and 2, in that specific musical constructions were investigated to discover the improvisation's building blocks and that verbal-assessment data were compared in relation to the therapeutic process as a whole, which are two different types of analysis. I believe the second analysis belongs to stage 4, in which the findings of stages 1 through 3 were compared and possible connections between the macro- and microanalyses were discussed. The therapeutic process as a whole (from stage 1) and the overall catalogue of musical components (from stage 2) were compared to the therapeutic and musical characteristics of sections of the improvisation. What seems missing in stage 3 is a comparison between the therapeutic and musical aspects within the sections of the improvisation.

In stage 5, the hypotheses are evaluated. The researcher–music therapist tested the first hypothesis against verbal data from the project as a whole. Two clients give evidence in favor of this hypothesis: one client stated on three occasions that the music was an accurate transcription of his development and the researcher–music therapist described the other as being aware of the benefits of relating music to his development. Surprisingly, testing this hypothesis does not seem to result in going through all research stages. What is more, the data used to verify this hypothesis are very limited. The second hypothesis is effect-oriented. The problem of internal validity is solved by letting the clients themselves describe how the music therapist's input affected their growth. This hypothesis focuses on particular improvisations, so it may be connected to stage 3, but it is unclear how the researcher–music therapist's analyses in stage 3 are connected to the client's own assessment of efficacy. Concerning the third hypothesis, the researcher tells us that each client used a generative cell that provided a basis for further musical development, which the clients experienced as connected to their illness. Finally, the researcher–music therapist verified the fourth hypothesis by the client's comments and small sections of the improvisations compared to precomposed music from different styles.

I think the problem with all the hypotheses is that the reader cannot verify whether and how validation resulted from the research stages and whether these stages were suitable for verifying these hypotheses. This type of research is qualitative, so it is unclear why Lee discusses the need to balance quantitative and qualitative aspects. What is quantitative in his research method? Is it the criterion of selecting sections of improvisations when more than one tape pause had been registered? We could quantify this criterion and point out that 50% of the participants paused at the same points if something important was happening. Lee does not provide arguments why the choices of two of four (50%) should merit making a particular selection.

The second and third criteria are also unclear. How were "evident density" and "richest amount of material" operationalized? There would have been two possibilities: to do it quantitatively, so that every other researcher would make the same selections, thus ensuring reliability, or to do it qualitatively, using member checks and peer debriefings. Although the researcher–music therapist used member checking (criterion 5), he did not use peer debriefing.

This research method seems somehow reductionistic to me. Although the researcher–music therapist develops an overall picture of the therapeutic process and the musical components in stages 1 and 2, the in-depth analysis is limited to two sections of one improvisation. Selection of small components can be used to verify hypotheses, but it cannot give a truly process-oriented picture. Perhaps this type of research resembles quantitative research because it also uses sampling.

STUDYING THE MUSICAL DIALOGUE
IN SINGLE-CASE PROCESS RESEARCH

Research in music therapy, according to Timmermann et al. (1991), must be process oriented, especially in describing and classifying the dialogue between the music therapist and the client. They identify audiovisual tapes of music therapy sessions as a means to replicate external observers' descriptions, defining this peer debriefing as a way to objectify. On the other hand, Timmermann et al. view the description of subjective phenomena in music therapy processes as being even more important. They conclude that because subjective phenomena are very difficult to describe, first things should be done first: objectification of the processes of interaction in music therapy should be the first focus of research. This way of thinking clearly shows that these researchers try to combine objective and subjective aspects and yet see no paradigmatic conflict in doing so. From another perspective, we might ask whether every method of objectification is not indeed a choice when we decide what is "objective," and whether the sequence of first researching the objective and then the subjective is not also a personal choice.

Timmermann et al. tried to answer two general questions:

- Is it possible to identify and to describe the typical musical dialogue in interactive music therapy? If it is possible, how can it be done ?
- Is it possible to describe this dialogue in words, or is it necessary to develop direct systems of notation?

They used two stages, described below, in trying to answer the two questions.

First Stage: Selecting Episodes

The distinct steps of the process of selection are as follows:

1. The music therapist and two colleagues (I will call the three of them the research team) intuitively selected short episodes from the video that they believed showed typical interaction patterns of the client.
2. The team discussed the episodes afterward. These discussions showed that their intuition had been led by the search for repetitions in rhythm, melody, and/or interaction or by the search for patterns of change, moments in which the client's expression and/or interaction with the therapist was clearly different.
3. Every team member verbally described every episode.
4. The team members discussed all descriptions and selected eight episodes, five of which illustrated repeti-

tive patterns and three of which were taken from the final session and reflected changes.

In the second stage, there were three groups of reviewers: music therapists, psychotherapists, and laypeople.

Second Stage: Reviewing Episodes

The aim of reviewing episodes was to search for some "general" meaning. Four questions guided this process:

1. Will the assessment of the client's personality by means of episodes be consistent with the clinical assessment?
2. Is it possible, as nonparticipants in treatment, to identify repetitive patterns when observing videotapes?
3. Will the assessment of interactional musical patterns by nonparticipants/non–music therapists be consistent with the music therapist's experience?
4. Is it possible for psychotherapists and laypeople to find these patterns?

The research team members developed a two-part questionnaire:

PART I. The first part of the questionnaire was to be completed for each episode and focused on how music therapist and client played the instruments, how they might have felt, and how they interacted. To investigate this, the team members used several tools:

- A list of 26 adjectives about moods and feelings (from Janke and Debus, 1971)
- A free description of the musical behavior to inventory concepts that can be of help in describing interaction
- Sentences that describe possible conflicts in the relationship; for instance, "The client wants attention" and "The client wants to dominate" (adapted from Luborsky and Kächele, 1988).
- A question about whether the role relationship was concordant or discordant (from Racker, 1968)

In this part of the questionnaire, generative concepts and deductive concepts, which have already been established, were combined. Another question was added so that the reviewers could note what they would have done if they had been the therapist (adapted from Strupp, 1960). This final question, however, deviates from the focuses of Part I.

PART II. The second part of the questionnaire, focused on general impressions, was composed of three questions:

1. How would you describe the client's personality?
2. What, in your opinion, is the client's primary problem?
3. What are the therapist's technical problems?

The questionnaire was given to 20 music therapists, 10 psychotherapists, and 20 laypeople to complete. The research team did content analysis and categorization of the free description. This part of the research was qualitative. Some of the categories found were isolation, schizoidism, problems of contact, being fixed, inhibition, inability to express feelings, and problems with self-esteem. The researchers concluded that the reviewers were able to assess the schizoid-narcissistic personality disorder from the musical material. The adjective list corroborated the free description. For instance, the category of schizoidism, developed in free description, corresponded to such adjectives as *juxtaposed, separated,* and *isolated.* Using different data-collecting methods (free description and adjective lists) can be interpreted as triangulation, which is an important tool in qualitative research.

The answers of the three rating groups (music therapists, psychotherapists, laypeople) were calculated statistically and showed no statistically significant differences. There was a trend, however, toward the psychotherapists having a stronger sense of psychopathology and the laypeople describing healthy aspects, with the music therapists falling somewhere in between. This trend is not surprising, because music therapists often combine two perspectives, the psychopathological and the creative.

Discussion

From the previous two stages it is obvious that it is possible to verbally describe the moods, feelings, musical behaviors, and musical dialogue between music therapist and client. Nevertheless, Timmermann et al. ask whether it is necessary to develop direct notation systems. They think that more sophisticated quantitative research requires a notation system specific to music therapy.

This brings us to a point that has been discussed quite often in the last few years by qualitative research. Music therapists from the Nordoff-Robbins school of music therapy use traditional notation because it is a universal language. A second reason is that, as Aldridge points out (1996a), Nordoff-Robbins music therapy originally made use of Rudolf Steiner's ideas about musical intervals, that when researcher–music therapists claim that each musical interval has a specific influence, they must notate intervals precisely. Although other anthroposophic music therapists likewise hold that effects result from specific intervals, rhythms, chords, and instruments, many Nordoff-Robbins music therapists today think differently because they contend that such a point of view denies the unique aspects of the improvisation and of perceptions of individual human beings. Qualitative music therapy researchers, who do not hold deterministic premises, argue that music therapy requires a different form of graphic notation that more clearly delineates its relevant aspects.

Langenberg, Frommer, and Langenbach (1996) have developed a graphic score. In my own research method, I use precise conventional notation when, as in my work with a musicogenic epileptic client, the amount and type of melodic intervals and rhythmic values is important. In treating many other clients, however, this precise conventional notation is neither necessary nor sufficient, so I use a combination of graphic notation and verbal musical concepts. To ensure trustworthiness, it is necessary to use some form of notation to check whether verbal interpretations are validated by musical data.

Timmermann et al. discuss three types of notation. Their first argument is that music therapy needs graphic notation because it is like "modern art" music, and traditional notation has shown shortcomings when scoring "modern art" music. The second argument is that a music therapy score should enable an independent reader to reproduce the musical interaction precisely.

In the replay rhythm score, there is a horizontal axis (the time axis) with two lines, one (the lowest) for the left hand and the other (the upper) for the right hand. The axis, on which 1 centimeter is 1 second in time, is used to graphically score a short episode. On two lines, graphic signs tell precisely when the client played and whether he or she played with a finger, a fist, curled fingers, or flat hand. The instruments and body posture are described in words. I find this score provides limited information on which dynamic changes occurred. How important is it to know whether the client played with a finger or flat hand? We might suppose that playing with a flat hand is louder, but this inference is inadequate because the client can play very loudly with a finger and very softly with a flat hand. What is really important to know is whether the client played softly or loudly. Thus, there is a difference between an operationalization score, which tells us which body parts were used, and a musical score, which tells us how it sounds. The signs for the same part of the hand differentiate playing strength somewhat, but I think the traditional terminology, which differentiates between piano, forte, and the nuances in between is much clearer. Of course, everybody can interpret *forte* differently, but the same is true for playing strength. Boldness is no perfect analogy for *loud,* so what is the difference between using the word *forte* or a bold graphic sign? Because the authors seek to enable a scholarly reader to reproduce the score, using the traditional words should not be a problem.

A second replay score for melody uses the same timetable but has five lines instead of two. The five lines resemble the traditional score, but the score is less precise: there is no key. For instance, I might see a slur between two pitches (a glissando). This slur could be quick, slow, between a high and a low pitch, between two high pitches or two low pitches, or go up or down. The point is that what I get from this score and what seems to be relevant for interpretation can also be described in traditional musical terms.

The so-called balk score is used to graphically represent a whole session. Now the timetable is different: 1 centimeter is 30 seconds. It is an interaction score that indicates how long the music therapist and the client played solo or together. It has been adopted from research in verbal psychotherapy. I have worked with precise time axes, as in a case involving musicogenic epilepsy. Now, however, I ask how important a precise timetable is. Does it really matter if we know exactly how long a client plays solo or together with the music therapist? Do we need such precise data? Sometimes these data look artificial: we see quantitative changes when there are no qualitative changes. Is it important that we know there is a difference of 5 seconds? Human beings are creatures that give meaning to their experiences. What is important to know is the meaning human beings give to these 5 seconds. We do not need to know the precise time lapse but whether it means something.

Again, it is apparent that the type of research developed by Timmermann et al. strives for "objectivity." When an independent observer analyzes the time axis precisely, he or she can calculate how long the client played solo or synchronously. So that the quantitative figures make sense, however, they are translated into qualitative language, saying, for instance, that in the beginning the client played for a very short time, then a very long time later, and that he did not play synchronously in the beginning but played synchronously later on. These qualitative definitions are further interpreted. We are given such interpretations as the client's expressiveness, creativity, or interaction increased. I do not think, however, that we need precise timetables to come to these conclusions. Perhaps they are only artificial positivistic fetishes. We can come to our qualitative conclusions through qualitative procedures.

The third score shows musical patterns, which are used to identify typical musical transformations. Again, I would ask what these patterns tell us about the client or therapy. Should we use both a musical score and terminology from human sciences, or should we try to describe the musical pattern in a language that already gives us psychological meaning? When explaining the musical score, Timmermann et al. use such musical terminology as *little intervals, part of scales, glissandi, thirds,* and so on. Again, we can conclude that what was scored graphically can also be put into words, but the therapeutic language we need is still missing. We need new terminology. I think the way Bruscia (1987) developed his "Improvisation Assessment Profiles" is a way out of this. He uses such concepts as integration, variability, tension, congruency, salience, and autonomy. To me, these words sound like the beginning of the intermediate language we need, because they can describe the psychic process in music, but Bruscia's profiles are very complex and difficult to handle. In my qualitative research experience, profiles are not as powerful as open descriptions given by several participants.

I would like to make some final comments. In the method of Timmermann et al., clients are not included during data analysis, so there is no member checking, but there are peer debriefings in which colleagues and other professionals are invited to react. New in this type of research is involving laypeople in the review process. As in other qualitative research, using panels enhances validation. Using laypeople adds something special, however: it shows that an important focus of this research effort is communication and understanding. In other words, can laypeople understand music therapy in a way that is significant to music therapists? When music therapists select important events, do laypeople also see these events as significant? In the work done by Timmermann et al., the research team preselected moments. The research would have had more power if other professionals and laypeople had been invited to select episodes themselves.

The concept of *category* has been used in a slightly different way than usual. In qualitative research, a category often is used like a box into which researchers put phrases that refer to aspects belonging to the same area of experience. For instance, *interaction, emotion,* and *body language* can be established as categories. The specific characteristics of those boxes give meaning to certain aspects of therapy. Sometimes this is called a theme or a motif. In the category *interaction,* describing the characteristics of interaction as *isolation, schizoidism,* and *problems of contact* gives meaning to the interaction, providing a theme or motif.

The research method is eclectic because preestablished measuring instruments are used together with open descriptions and concepts are deduced and generated at the same time. The question for which the reviewers could describe what they would have done if they had been the therapist illustrates that this research method also has characteristics of action research. In action research, the researcher or reviewers are invited in peer debriefings to develop alternative strategies and influence the course of treatment. That final question, however, is not pure action research, because by the time it is posed, treatment has already ended and the alternative strategies cannot be of benefit for that particular treatment.

MEANINGFUL EPISODES

Definitions

The Integrative Music Therapy Documentation System (IMDoS) was developed at the Department of Music Therapy in the Fachhochschule Heidelberg in Germany. IMDoS in essence is a computer program that collects, categorizes, and analyzes information. It serves several purposes, such as case administration, music therapy research, music therapy education, and assessment and improvement of treatment quality. Its underlying philosophy is the integration of research, treatment, and education. Clients are assessed in conventional ways, but episodes from significant treatment events are also videotaped. The video episode can be part of both research and education; however, I will focus only on the research aspect here.

The researchers from the IMDoS team are aware of the difficulties inherent in studying the clinical setting. They describe conventional research as, for instance, being focused on "laws," randomizing participants into groups, being long term, and eliminating subjectivity in favor of objectivity. In treatment, however—according to the researchers—the individual is the focus, clients are selected to be part of treatment groups, decisions have to be made quickly, and subjectivity is essential. We can see some of the same aspects emphasized by several qualitative researchers. Because of the difference between research and clinical practice, the IMDoS researchers want to develop a research strategy that produces results close to those obtained clinically.

This connection to clinical practice is shaped by an integration of quantitative and qualitative aspects, which has three fundamental aspects:

- All therapeutic treatments are assessed by pretests, post-tests, and process measurements. This aspect is quantitative.

- The results of process measurements are handed over, during treatment, to the music therapist, who can then reflect on, continue, or change his or her style of treatment.

    This technique resembles action research, because the research process influences the treatment process, and member checking, although not the type typical of qualitative research, because the music therapist obtains "objective" data he or she can use. At this stage, the music therapist's perspective is not included so that the credibility of his or her assessments can be verified.

- Instead of studying the final effects of music therapy by quantitative or qualitative means, the third aspect focuses on process: the conditions and situations leading to the effects. Describing conditions resembles grounded theory. To establish conditions, the researchers choose Greenberg's "episode paradigm" (1986), which, in their opinion, produces empirical evidence and is close to clinical thinking.

    I wonder, however, whether working with episodes should be called a paradigm because a paradigm is a much more basic epistemology. For a discussion of critical episodes, see also van Colle and Williams (1995). The therapist's and client's subjective perspectives are taken as a starting point for analysis. The clinician searches for aspects of his or her treatment behavior that seem important but are preconscious because they were not part of his or her professional education. The researchers analyze and interpret the subjective perspectives. Although these analyses can be done in several quantitative and qualitative ways, the fact that they are conducted in a naturalistic setting and use feedback to enhance the therapist's awareness makes them close to the qualitative research paradigm.

In episode research it is supposed that therapeutic progress is not continuous, but that there are critical points at which development is manifested. Episodes are clinically significant units.

Selection

The researchers state that in general, episodes are selected by qualitative and quantitative means, by self-reports and measuring instruments from music therapists and clients. Episodes can be defined in three ways:

1. Qualitatively:
   A. A moment that someone subjectively experiences as meaningful
   B. A moment that a client signifies, by means of preestablished categories, as meaningful.
2. Quantitatively: A moment that fits the description given by a measuring instrument

In 1A, only the music therapist is asked, after each session, to signify which events were important. The client's perspective is not included. The episodes are limited to 1 minute each, but several are allowed. We might ask whether this time limitation is too artificial and reduces meaningful processes. After making the selection, the music therapist gives qualitative descriptions of the chosen episodes. This part of the research method might be enhanced by including the client's choice or those of other participants. The reason I make this point is that if the researchers want to find blind spots, depending completely on the music therapist's choice can introduce bias.

The chosen episodes are used as a basis for further analyses. Students write qualitative descriptions of each episode and analyze them by means of measuring instruments, discussed below. Whereas the selection of episodes involves only the therapist's perspective, this stage adds observers' perspectives. I am curious as to why multiple perspectives are used in the second stage but not the first stage. The researchers try to develop a database of episodes reflecting the structure, process, and type of each episode. The qualitative descriptions are used to develop categories and the quantitative figures are used to develop "dimensions" of episodes. Finally, episodes are indexed and can be used in education.

Measuring instruments have been developed to measure psychological (MUSIKOS), musical (MUERB), and behavioral (HEIN) aspects in the musical dialogue.

HEIN. The behavioral measurement (HEIN: Heidelberg Episode Inventory) consists of 32 items, including body posture, verbal style, opposition, empathy, openness, self-exploration, and musical play. Factor analysis of the measuring instrument produced four factors: verbal opposition versus musical cooperation, nonverbal expressiveness and making contact, verbal self-expression and self-evaluation, and affective-cognitive involvement.

MUSIKOS. The MUSIKOS (Music Therapy Coding System) instrument is a semantic differential. It also underwent factor analysis, which found two factors: activity and closeness. It uses 10 bipolar items: confident/not confident, resolute/indecisive, relaxed/tense, active/passive, expressive/reserved, lively/calm, friendly/unfriendly, turned toward/turned away, warm/cold, emotional/unemotional.

Single-Case Studies

The factorial structures have been used in single-case studies. Here, we will concentrate on one example from Czogalik et al. (1995) involving a man diagnosed as schizophrenic with manic-depressive episodes. Later on, a postpsychotic syndrome was also diagnosed. His parents divorced, which increased the ambivalence of his relationship to his mother and resulted in an ambivalent, dependent relationship to other people, especially women. The client was very vulnerable, but during music therapy his self-esteem and reality test scores increased. His ability to cope with conflicts and be authentic improved because in music therapy he explored how to express and experience feelings. Anxieties connected to loss and insecurity about the future were integrated. Therapy was conducted by two student cotherapists supervised by one music therapist from the teaching course (E. W. Selle).

It had been asked whether HEIN's factorial structure could adequately reflect individual cases, whether it could produce a valid qualitative "description" of the episodes, and whether its four factors could produce a summary of the process from session episode to session episode. Twenty-eight sessions were part of the research. From each session, the music therapists chose one episode. There were four student observers who scored each episode's videotape using HEIN. A fifth student wrote an open description.

Means of the four students' scores for each item were calculated. For every episode, there were 32 item means for the music therapists and 32 for the client. These items were categorized into groups along the factorial structure that had resulted from the previous factor analysis and were combined in four factorial scores. For each factor, the factorial scores for all 28 episodes were graphed to show how a particular factor changed from episode to episode.

Statistics (Cronbach's alpha) showed a moderate internal consistency of factors (0.76, 0.57, 0.48, 0.64). The researchers concluded that the factorial structure therefore adequately reflects the individual case. Further analyses showed that in the graph of the factor "verbal opposition versus musical cooperation," the scores of cotherapists and client were very close to musical cooperation. For the factor of "nonverbal expressiveness and making contact," there were episodes in which the client's graphed line differed from the cotherapists' factorial scores. Sometimes the client's nonverbal expression and contact was stronger than the cotherapists'. For the factor of "verbal self-expression and self-evaluation," the client's factorial score for most episodes was higher; the client was more verbally expressive and provided more self-evaluation. For the factor of "affective-cognitive involvement," the cotherapists' scores were most often higher. The researchers interpreted these findings as follows:

- Factor 1 shows that for music therapy, musical cooperation is typical.
- Factor 2 shows that the music therapists do not always take the client up on his offer of close contact.

- Factor 3 shows that the music therapists are not using many verbal techniques.
- Factor 4 shows that there is strong affective-cognitive involvement by the music therapists.

In the interpretations, there are two lines of reasoning. The first one tries to provide general characteristics of music therapy, such as musical cooperation is typical in music therapy, musical interventions precede verbal interventions in music therapy, and music therapy is indicated whenever verbal expression is disturbed. The second line of reasoning, which results from the combination of music therapy research and training, makes it difficult to decide, however, whether interpretations reflect music therapy in general or music therapy training. For instance, is there less contact (factor 2) because the students cannot handle the situation or is it typical in music therapy, with this type of client, for music therapists keep a distance? In factor 3, do the students—as the researchers themselves argue—lack verbal abilities or did the students not want to reinforce the client's pathological verbal behavior or is it typical of music therapy that there is more musical than verbal interaction? The three possible explanations have different focuses: training, the client's disturbance, and music therapy in general. The reasoning used for the fourth factor is similar. The researchers ask themselves whether the students did not succeed—because of lack of experience—in reaching an attitude of engaged distance or whether they wanted to increase affective dynamics. This final aspect shows a lack of member checking. The student music therapists themselves could easily have explained their intentions had they been asked.

Let us return to the second question the researchers asked: was this measuring instrument able to give a valid qualitative "description" of the episodes? What we actually get are reductionistic factor scores telling us whether there is musical cooperation, nonverbal expressiveness and contact, verbal self-expression and self-evaluation, and affective-cognitive involvement. These factors are important, but they are abstract and limited and contribute little to our understanding of the psychodynamic processes of music therapy. The same holds true for the description of the process these factors produce. As I put it before, quantitative research can tell us something specific about what is going on by using hard figures, but it does not produce a holistic description. I would ask all the phenomenologists out there whether these factors give us the essence of music therapy.

In this single-case study, the researchers conclude that qualitative data give information that cannot be gained through quantitative data and vice versa, and that quantitative and qualitative research can and should therebfore be combined. In another single-case study (Vanger et al., 1995), in which the MUSIKOS measurement instrument was used, the researchers conclude that the reduced quantitative analyses were congruent with the music therapist's qualitative holistic descriptions. The first argument, that quantitative research gives different data from that produced by qualitative research and vice versa, is in line with the basic axioms of qualitative research. The second argument, that the results of quantitative and qualitative research are congruent, depends on how we define *congruent*. Reducing data means that they are incorporated in what is reduced, but reduced data cannot replace holistic descriptions.

Chapter 13

A CONTINUING DIALOGUE

Qualitative Music Therapy Research: Beginning Dialogues (1996, edited by Langenberg, Aigen, and Frommer) was a result of the Düsseldorf symposium. In it, each symposium presenter wrote a monologue and then a dialogue in which he or she reacted to colleagues' monologues. This taught me a lot, including the fact that my own position on qualitative research is disputed. The reason is clear: I use such "old" concepts as "reliability" and "validity," but researchers influenced by the work of Yvonna Lincoln and Egon Guba reject these terms. I felt a bit like a Don Quixote, trying to defend medieval chivalrous values despite changing times. I gave it a lot of thought and concluded that in the end, there are a lot of points on which my colleagues and I agree, such as not interfering with the natural course of treatment and using both our own and participants' subjectivity to give meaning to the humanness of music therapy. To stress this agreement in this book, I have put such terms as *reliability* and *validity* within quotation marks ("reliability," "validity").

Perhaps the ambiguity within which my colleagues perceive my methods belies the very strength of my epistemological position, but I still believe that the "medieval" research concepts can be transformed into concepts that adequately describe qualitative research. They can span the river of our ever-changing experiences and tie the knight with the quantitative countenance to the sirens who sing seductive qualitative songs. Do not misunderstand the criticisms I make in this book. I very deeply respect my colleagues' work, much of which I inspires me. I have tried here to describe their methods as adequately as possible, but I also gave commented and critiqued from my own perspective. Some readers will agree with me; others will not. From Düsseldorf and the events that followed it, I learned that music therapy researchers can have fundamental disagreements and still respect one another's work. This is one of the metavalues of our dialogues. For our clients' benefit, we must maintain this openness and respect.

In this final chapter, I will first summarize and categorize some of the qualitative research perspectives described in the previous chapters. Then I will continue the dialogue we began during the 1994 qualitative research symposium in Düsseldorf and continued through the 1996 conference in Berlin and the 1996 World Congress of Music Therapy in Hamburg. Finally, I will list the themes I believe to be fundamental to continuing this discussion.

QUALITATIVE RESEARCH IN MUSIC THERAPY: AN OVERALL PICTURE

I will first provide a short summary of the different qualitative research approaches.

New Paradigm

Some researchers, such as Michele Forinash, David Gonzalez, Ken Aigen, Dorit Amir, Carolyn Kenny, and Rosemarie Tüpker, use a completely new paradigm, as do Lincoln and Guba. They hold their concepts and procedures to be fundamentally different from those of quantitative research. Forinash and Gonzalez (1989) reject quantitative research because they believe it cannot explain the essence of music therapy. One of the sources they use to describe this essence is music therapists' personal experiences. They believe that subjectivity should be a research instrument. Aigen (1996a, 1996b) uses the music therapist's subjective and empathic experiences to describe the client's subjectivity in constructs. In her research, Kenny (1996a, 1996b) concluded that efforts to quantify her music therapy work were useless. She thinks we should not reduce phenomena by using prefixed theories, variables, and frequencies but should instead describe phenomena from the participants' perspective and concentrate on aesthetic and existential experiences left out by quantitative methods. Tüpker (1990)—like Lincoln and Guba—discusses the traditional research criteria, such as replicability, objectivity and empiricism. She concludes that replicability is impossible, that objectivity in situations where people meet is biased, and that the experimental setting splits a holistic phenomenon into a number of variables.

Modified New Paradigm

Other researchers, such as Ken Bruscia, Hanna Schirmer, Axel Hupfeld, Mechtild Langenberg, Jörg Frommer, Michael Langenbach, and Isabelle Frohne-Hagemann, use methods close to the previously mentioned ones in some aspects but not in others. Bruscia (1995a, 1995b, 1996a, 1996b) describes how he, as a music therapist, goes back and forth between different spheres of consciousness. He holds that music therapists can focus their consciousness on their clients' worlds, on their own personal world, or on their worlds as music therapists. Bruscia is less radical, however, when he states that qualitative research also needs some basic rules. Langenberg, Frommer, and Langenbach (1996) developed the concept of a resonator function in which clients, music therapists, and observers, using prefixed categories, spontaneously give their impressions when listening to a musical improvisation. This perspective differs from an open qualitative approach because categories are developed beforehand. In the content analysis—when developing motifs—these researchers aim for intersubjectivity, not multiple subjectivity. Schirmer and Hupfeld (1988) replace objectivity with the objectification of subjective impressions. They are looking for consensus of meaning in individual associations. Frohne-Hagemann (1995) uses the term *sections of experiences*. In her opinion, reality (objectivity) develops by relating and the consensus that comes from it.

Qualitative and Quantitative Methods in the Same Project

Other researchers, such as Tonius Timmermann, Nicola Scheytt-Hölzer, Suzanne Bauer, Horst Kächele, Christian Remmert, and David Aldridge, try to bridge the discrepancy between qualitative and quantitative research. Timmermann et al. (1991) stress that the objective approach should not be the only one and that describing subjective phenomena is important. They use a combination of qualitative and quantitative methodologies, as does Remmert (1992). This perspective is very different from that of qualitative researchers, such Aigen and Kenny, who think that qualitative and quantitative paradigms are so different that they cannot be used at the same time in one research project. Aldridge (1996a) emphasizes the validation of measuring instruments. He sees the single-case study as a tool that can be used at the start of a research process, with qualitative and quantitative projects as sequential steps because they complement each other.

Qualitative and Quantitative Methods for Different Projects

My own research method is characterized above all by the cooperation of music therapist and researcher—with different people in each role—during treatment (Smeijsters and van den Hurk 1993, 1994, in press; Smeijsters and van den Berk, 1995; Smeijsters and Storm, 1997). I do not advocate combining qualitative and quantitative research in the same project, but I believe that a qualitative researcher can also be a quantitative researcher and that we need both qualitative and quantitative research projects. I do not think that the existential perspective of the qualitative researcher disqualifies him or her as a quantitative researcher or vice versa. Although I have adapted Lincoln and Guba's research techniques, I use transformations of the traditional concepts of "validity" and "reliability."

DIALOGUES

In this section, I will not repeat verbatim the presentations of the speakers at the Düsseldorf symposium (Aigen, Smeijsters, Kenny, Bruscia, Amir, and Langenberg, Frommer, and Langenbach) because these were published in another book (*Qualitative Music Therapy Research: Beginning Dialogues*, 1996) and I have already referred to them in this book. Instead, I will concentrate on the discussions in Düsseldorf and on the dialogues written afterward as feedback to the monologues. The dialogues were also included in *Qualitative Music Therapy Research*.

My description here of the discussion and ongoing dialogue is personal. I made no effort to make it "objective" by excluding the names of those contributing to the discussions and dialogues because discussions and dialogues are exchanges between people about their own beliefs and doubts within their personal context of reference. On the other hand, I do not mean to give more weight to what they are saying by mentioning their names. When we hold a discussion, we should listen to what our discussion partners are telling us, without being biased by prestige, and try to understand what they are communicating, respecting their views even when these are contrary to our own and expressing our beliefs, doubts, and insecurities without fear of abandonment. What I learned from Düsseldorf and Hamburg and the dialogues that followed them is that we can indeed have fruitful academic discussions.

At the end of this section, I will include some ideas and comments from such qualitative researchers as Aldridge, Even Ruud, and Penny Rogers, who were present in Düsseldorf and made contributions to qualitative research in their own publications. In all this, the primary focus is an open dialogue about my own position and those of my colleagues.

During the Düsseldorf symposium, Aigen (1996a) said that qualitative research needs specific values that can be transformed into specific criteria for research. He believes that the personal and contextual should be one of the fundamental values, the personal no longer being disqualified as an obstacle to research. To me, this position is an understandable one for American researchers. They emphasize the personal now because for decades, quantitative behavioral methods were favored. It also occurs to me that this position is a result of the fact that when music therapists themselves become researchers, they transfer their therapeutic attitude to the research setting. Aigen defines doing research as a process of selecting data that corroborate the researcher's own ideas. If, according to him, the researcher uses *I* when writing about his or her research, the reader knows that he or she made personal selections and decisions. The researcher does not claim "truth" and "objectivity" but gives personal meaning to the data. Aigen also makes a distinction between guidelines and rules for research. He believes that in qualitative research, there can be no rules, only guidelines.

In the discussion following Aigen's presentation at Düsseldorf, some researchers thought there was confusion concerning values, believing that qualitative research needs values beyond "respecting the personal and contextual." There also was a discussion about how far a researcher can go in being personal and subjective. Some asked whether there is a real danger that the researcher can be absorbed by the personal. In his dialogue in *Qualitative Music Therapy Research* (1996b), Aigen confesses that he had not understood my position clearly in my presentation in Düsseldorf when I spoke about the concepts of "reliability" and "validity." But hearing my statement that my thinking is still developing and changing showed him that my position is a "personal" one. As I said at the beginning of this section, the "personal" point of view, not excluding our own subjectivity and not trying to hide behind the mask of "objectivity," makes it possible to be open to each other and to have a scientific "I and thou" discourse. When Aigen heard my personal statement, this—in his own words—"rendered [him] more able to *hear* [me]". The personal statement enhanced his trust in me because it showed him that I am searching and not promoting myself as a quantitative warrior defending old territory and attacking new ones. Aigen made a personal statement, too. In his dialogue, he asked himself why he had chosen the topic of values. He went back to his roots in Judaism, in which social justice—giving all people a voice—plays an important role. Such techniques as member checking can be inferred from this. Other researchers come to this point through their own cultural and political background. In any case, this line of reasoning is very different from traditional research, in which the researcher is a powerful autocrat who, by using research instruments and through the *Verdinglichung* of

the participants, develops theories "about" people. As Max Horkheimer, Theodor Adorno, Martin Heidegger, Paul Feyerabend,
and others pointed out, this type of research makes science an
instrument of control.

Aigen is very open when delving into his unconscious
motives. He comes to the conclusion that in choosing "values" as a
topic of investigation, he unconsciously was placing himself in a
morally superior position. Perhaps his own need to moralize was
activated when he was listening to my attempt at using the old
research concepts. To me, his openness feels very trustworthy. It
brings me one step further and forces me to ask myself again: why
am I advocating the use of the old terms? Could it be that I want
to be accepted by quantitative researchers? Do I want to
"Christianize" qualitative researchers? In any case, Aigen's
dialogue convinced me that my attitude as a qualitative researcher is very close to that of some of my colleagues.

Several other researchers also commented that such
concepts as "reliability" and "validity" inadequately describe the
characteristics of qualitative research. Amir (1996b) even wrote in
her dialogue that my paper left her frustrated. This shows how
personally researchers may react when they feel their paradigm is
questioned. This phenomenon—a group of researchers countering
someone else's position—in my opinion illustrates Thomas Kühn's
concept of *paradigm* (1975). When there is an insecurity about the
previously held beliefs regarding scientific progress, scientists
adopt a new belief that gives them hope that unsolved problems
may be solved. A scientific revolution—a shift of paradigm—takes
place when scientists decide there should be one. Scientific
progress in itself is "qualitative": it is not an immovable law of
progress but depends on beliefs, choices, perspectives, and constructs. After a scientific revolution has taken place, the old
theories and concepts are abandoned.

In music therapy research, the quantitative perspective
that was used for many years was undermined by music therapists' experience that this paradigm could not describe the
"essence" of music therapy. Music therapists who wanted to study
their own clinical practice adopted Lincoln and Guba's qualitative
paradigm.

Discussing one's own beliefs with a group of researchers who
all share beliefs belonging to another paradigm can be difficult.
Sometimes I have felt like a stranger in someone else's cosmos. I am

neither an advocate of the quantitative paradigm nor a full adept of the qualitative paradigm. In my professional development, I have been guided by a belief that there might be a third paradigm. In Chapter 3 of this book, I explained my belief that quantitative and qualitative research methods are guided by the same four scientific principles defined by Lincoln and Guba (1985):

- The "truth" of the findings for the respondents
- The degree to which findings may apply to other contexts
- The replicability of the findings
- The degree to which the findings stem from the respondents' characteristics and not the inquirer's biases

Bruscia and Aldridge also see some advantage in using the "old" concepts because doing so makes possible discussions between qualitative and quantitative researchers. In Düsseldorf, this brought us to a discussion about the language we should use when communicating about music therapy, a very old but nevertheless important topic. Some researchers argue that we need a new language to describe music therapy, while others maintain that whatever language we use, it must be understandable by people outside music therapy with whom we communicate. Aldridge said that building bridges and entering into dialogues within the field music therapy and between music therapy and other clinical fields is very necessary. He used the metaphor of two people starting at different places and digging the ends of a tunnel that must meet in the middle. They can succeed only if they can communicate. If they both speak different languages, then the parts of the tunnel will never meet because they cannot explain their own positions on the map by using the other person's meridians. Although they are in different positions, they need a shared system of meridians. Aigen expanded the bridge metaphor, saying that the researcher is the material for the bridge.

Aldridge's perspective is close to my belief that there are some basic scientific questions universal to both quantitative and qualitative research. I am sure, however, that other qualitative researchers will argue that both groups' using the same system of meridians is impossible. I think we need bridges between quantitative and qualitative research and also between music therapists and psychiatrists, psychologists, psychotherapists, pediatricians, medical doctors, and scientists. The language of music therapy should not be esoteric, for music therapists only. It should make it possible for us to communicate with other clinicians not in their vocabulary but in one that expresses the essence of music therapy and explains its connections to the other areas. I would call it an in-between language in which the musical processes are encoded as psychic processes.

One related question concerns how to score musical improvisation. In most qualitative research methods, thoughts, images, feelings, values, associations, stories, adjectives, symbols, and memories are written down, but there is no musical score. When there is a musical score, as Rogers says, there are few research studies that "directly approach the central difficulty of making a verbal analysis of an essentially musical event" (Rogers, 1993). In Düsseldorf, there was a discussion of whether a new musical notation is needed. Aldridge, as a representative of the Nordoff-Robbins method, expressed his opinion that classical musical notation should be used because it is universal and understandable to everyone. I would say that because in Nordoff-Robbins music therapy all types of songs play an important role, classical notation is appropriate. Musical improvisation is different, though. From my own experience, I know that classical notation does not capture the essence of the musical-psychosocial processes that occur during improvisation. On the basis of my concept of *analogy* (Smeijsters, 1996a), I would advocate a new notation that would illustrate the psychic and social processes. As I have said before, Bruscia's assessment profiles can be very useful here. Other researchers at the Düsseldorf symposium, including Michael Langenbach and Benedikte Barth-Scheiby, expressed doubt about the appropriateness of classical notation and advocated a new graphic score.

In her Düsseldorf monologue, Kenny (1996a) described how she gradually felt the necessity to find a new language to describe music therapy and the impressions and expressions it gives us. She advocates the participants' perspectives and concentrates on the aesthetic and the free fantasy variation. In her opinion, human beings create fictions, such as music, to construct their understanding of reality. Like Aigen, she believes the research method should be appropriate to the research topic. "If we think of creativity as being important, how is it possible to do quantitative research?" she argues. She acknowledges, however, that researchers need some handhold to satisfy their need for security. At the end of her monologue, she includes a great perspective of being healthy: knowing a lot of songs to sing.

One intriguing question Bruscia asked during the discussion of Kenny's presentation was "Why are we researching?" At the time, I answered, "To understand what is happening." Now, however, I ask myself, "What does it mean to 'understand'?" Aigen's answer to Bruscia's question was "I am doing research because I like it." Bruscia's answer was "To become more conscious." Aigen's answer seemed very egocentric to me at the time. Another interpretation has since occurred to me: he who is doing his work because he likes it has no other interests. Perhaps this is an important condition of being authentic (an issue discussed more later in this section). Barbara Wheeler felt it important to experience and be touched when doing research. I agree that as a researcher, we cannot "understand" human beings if we do not experience.

In her monologue, Kenny wrote that she wants to screen out the last remnants of the positivistic paradigm: language, concepts, assumptions, values, cause and effect, and so on. This makes her a strong advocate of the qualitative paradigm. She classifies my attempt to use such criteria as "validity" and "reliability" as in line with the natural sciences. This shows me that what I was trying to communicate has been misunderstood. This is why Amir was frustrated; she also saw my ideas as positivistic. Ruud (1996b, 1996c) sees my way of thinking as a methodological one, finding new methods to fulfill "old" criteria, but he believes it might be really a problem of epistemology and not of methodology.

When I talk about "validity" and "reliability," my intention is neither to use the technical operationalizations of the natural sciences and positivism, nor to use the traditional definitions of *validity* and *reliability*. What I called "describing new contents for old concepts" I think not only refers to the methodological aspect but also respects the different epistemology of qualitative research. Nevertheless, Ruud's argument forces me to reflect on whether the idea of basic research questions, even when their constituents are defined differently, can indeed reflect qualitative epistemology. Perhaps these questions also belong to positivistic epistemology; if so, then it would be necessary to reformulate them.

In the opinion of Langenbach and Stratkötter (1996), qualitative and quantitative research are not two completely different, mutually exclusive worlds. Instead of criticizing my ideas like other qualitative researchers do by saying that I should accept that qualitative and quantitative research are mutually exclusive, Langenbach and Stratkötter are telling me that I should acknowledge that they are not mutually exclusive. This illustrates the problem of walking on the bridge between two worlds: for some people, it is too far from the left shore, and for others, it is too far from the right. In fact, Langenbach and Stratkötter criticize all my arguments about the differences between qualitative and quantitative research. More specifically, they criticize my contention that qualitative research is closer to experience. They think I use a simple knowledge–truth model, believing that qualitative research gives us representational knowledge, even though there is always transformation and interpretation. To me, this criticism is beside the point. As a qualitative researcher, I do not claim that qualitative research gives us more "truth," because "truth" is a concept that cannot be used in qualitative research. On the contrary, I admit that there is always interpretation. What I mean by saying that qualitative research is closer to experience is that there are fewer distancing levels of interpretation and less abstraction. Experiencing a phenomenon yourself, the way the music therapist/researcher experiences the music and the client during music therapy, differs from listening/looking at the tape, using words to describe what has happened, and reducing phenomena to variables and figures, as in quantitative research. Using items and scoring them as in quantitative research is a way of making phenomena "objective," at the same time excluding many personal processes you experience when in the phenomenon yourself. I do not agree with Langenbach and Stratkötter's claim that qualitative researchers are interested in "subjective experiences" and quantitative researchers are interested in "experiences of general laws." Most qualitative researchers come to the conclusion that "general laws" developed in quantitative research are unable to give us what we experience as the essence of music therapy. Experiences and general laws are mutually exclusive.

"Openness" in qualitative research means adjusting your research method to the unique natural context, whereas in quantitative research, the natural context is adjusted to prefixed categories deduced from existing theory so that tests can be used. As Aldridge (1996a) puts it, measuring instruments are precise, fixed procedures that give us stable and definite empirical content, and imaginative life studies are less precise but maintain a close relationship with the natural social world of people. As a researcher myself, I know that I am taking a very different position when I use standardized measuring instruments that register observable variables than when I am myself the "instrument." Of course, it all depends on how you define *experience*. For Langenbach and Stratkötter, a "general law" of music therapy can be "experienced" the way being part of a music therapy experience can be "experienced." For me, however, these are different types of experiences, the improvisation being closer to the phenomenon, the general law about the improvisation being more distanced from it.

Frommer (1997) says that there are two categories of qualitative researchers: those who, like Kenny, want to abandon every resemblance to quantitative research and those who feel there is some common ground left between the quantitative and qualitative paradigm. Although I am a representative of the second category, what strikes me is that I came to the same conclusions about qualitative research as Kenny and others. Langenberg, an analytical therapist, confronted me in one of our discussions with the possibility that I am searching for agreements because I might have an unconscious personal wish to be part of the new-paradigm group. I reflected on Langenberg's idea and concluded that my position is an expression of a mild intrapsychic conflict between two value systems. Looking back on my scientific development, I see an ongoing balancing between traditional scientific values and my affiliation with humanistic psychology and the critical theory of the Frankfurt school. These aspects represent areas of my personality: being gifted in statistics as a boy and student, being a humanistic therapist and teacher, and being a critical theorist. It might be easier to jump into the qualitative paradigm completely instead of searching for a connection between paradigms that may be incompatible, but I would feel inauthentic solving my epistemological problem by completely abandoning the quantitative paradigm.

In Düsseldorf, Bruscia (1996a) advocated allowing the music therapist to also serve as the researcher. To guard against mixing these roles, he starts his research when therapy has finished. He introduced countertransference as a research tool. In an earlier article, Tüpker (1990a, 1990b) also discussed this topic. Bruscia introduced such perspectives as having the same feelings as the client, adjusting one's own feelings to the client's feelings (accommodating), and putting the client's feelings within one's personal frame of reference (assimilating). He describes research as "bringing to consciousness what is on the threshold of consciousness." In his opinion, the therapist's countertransference can occur on different levels; thus, reflecting one's own countertransference is very important. I think the researcher's so-called controlled subjectivity (Tüpker) is a necessary but insufficient condition for qualitative research.

Bruscia also dealt with the concept of authenticity and the value of researchers themselves having feelings of authenticity. No one else, according to Bruscia, can judge a person's authenticity. One has to be continuously aware of such questions as:

- Am I still focusing on the same topic?
- Context: What are my personal motives?
- Method: Are there enough data?
- Findings: Am I as open as possible for unexpected findings?
- Communication: What will I be communicating about the research?

Bruscia asked himself whether *countertransference* and *authenticity* are the right terms to use. I would like to comment on the latter term. Bruscia is right nobody else really can judge someone else's authenticity, an inner process that only can be guessed from the outside. We feel our own inauthenticity, our own existential guilt inside; however, this gives us many problems when we are doing research. It seems Bruscia is saying that verifying research procedures and results is made much simpler by asking the researcher "Do you feel you are being authentic?" and then closing the discussion. This cannot be the proper way for researchers to communicate, so perhaps this is not really what Bruscia is saying. For Kenny, authenticity is a "body sense." Just as it is difficult to put music into words, she says, it is difficult to have a mental construct for authenticity. In his dialogue, Aigen gives us another solution: believe the person who demonstrates some capacity for self-knowledge and self-criticism. The word *demonstrates* is key, I believe. Although demonstrating is an expression of inwardly felt authenticity, we need this exteriorization. It is not enough when somebody tells us that he or she is authentic, that he or she has achieved self-knowledge and self-criticism. Researchers can ensure trustworthiness only by manifesting it themselves. Kenny also mentions revealing underlying assumptions, values, beliefs, and so on.

I therefore subscribe to the concept of the chain of evidence that makes it possible for a colleague to verify authenticity because research values and decisions, feelings, thoughts, insights, and so on, are expressed in the research report. As we saw in Chapter 9, this is what Bruscia is doing. Aigen, however, wrote in his dialogue that he thinks it is an impossible task to become our colleagues' "authenticity police." He replaces the intersubjective standard with an intrasubjective one. Nevertheless, he wants to share his struggles with others.

In his dialogue, Bruscia describes my perspective as being like the person who, when traveling with his colleagues through a labyrinth, takes a compass and a book. The compass tells him in which direction he is walking within the labyrinth. The book contains maps of all the labyrinths ever built—save the labyrinth he is in now. This is indeed a very good description of me. I feel a need to decipher the scriptures of music therapy, to incorporate all existing maps and determine where we are and where we are going, to show my students and colleagues how to find their way out of the "labyrinth." In the books and articles I have written, I was always busy making "maps of the territory." More recently, however, my professional need to be released from these maps and compasses, to incorporate change, walking ahead and "listening" and trusting my own senses, has increased. This need is also a very personal one. I love going for a walk in a forest. I often decide beforehand whether I will be "walking on the map" or trying to find a way out without any instruments. Years ago, I discovered that if I trust my intuition, I always find a way out. Likewise, before I studied the literature on qualitative research, I found that the person can indeed be the instrument.

Amir (1996a) made a presentation in Düsseldorf about her doctoral research (also described in this book). She, too, views the researcher as the most important "instrument"; like Aigen, she was doing research to find her own "truth," being as open as possible. In all these perspectives (Aigen, Bruscia, and Amir), there is a researcher who makes personal choices, wants to be open, and decides whether that openness is authentic. For me, it is difficult to understand how in research we can check these intrapsychic processes. They are all in the researcher's psyche. Does this research approach mean that a researcher needs to be a fully functioning person? If so, who can tell us that he or she is—the researcher him- or herself? Amir's presentation resulted in an energetic discussion. Aigen pointed out that Amir had told us that she wanted her theory to come from the participants, but she had used selective sampling. Did she use it because she expected that some participants would support her theory more than others? Bruscia asked whether in the interviews she used the concept of meaningful moments. Amir's answer was that she did not because she did not want to stimulate the respondents' desire for social acceptance. Bruscia argued that telling what we are asking for enhances authenticity. In his dialogue, Aigen is very open about this discussion with Amir. He tells us that he felt as if he was scapegoating Amir. I did not perceive it that way, but maybe some other participants felt the same tension Aigen did. I think his comment on this is significant because the self-criticism in the end makes the discussion trustworthy.

Langenberg, Frommer, Langenbach (1996) described their method of qualitative research (also described in this book). Some of the American qualitative researchers are searching not for intersubjectivity (agreements on meanings) but for multiple subjectivities that supplement each other. There is no section of agreed meanings.

In the final discussion in Düsseldorf, there were other personal topics mentioned. Kenny felt that in the future, such aspects as aesthetic, holism, space, intuition, and culture should be developed further. Ruud thought it important to use metaphors in research. Frommer expressed his satisfaction about the fact that in qualitative psychotherapy research, the distinction between psychotherapeutic schools is fading away. There were other contributions to the discussion that were published independently of the Düsseldorf forum, however, some by members of this forum.

Aldridge (1996a) wrote that not everything is measurable in numbers. His question of how to "measure" emotion shows us the problem of measuring a phenomenon that will be influenced by the measurement itself. I would like to add to this that measuring such a complexity as an emotion means measuring something about the emotion, not the emotion. What is then measured is an abstraction of it, or as Aldridge puts it, we are then separating data from people, classifying and analyzing people as "cases" when "in reality, we are working with individuals that are suffering . . ." (Aldridge, 1996b).

While I am writing this book as support for my own ideas, I realize that my work on indications relies strongly on reducing people to "vessel[s] for the containment of a disease" (Aldridge, 1996a). This makes me ambivalent. My intention was to adjust music therapy to specific diseases and to ask myself "Why and how can music therapy contribute to improvement of schizophrenia, depression, anorexia, or borderline . . . ?" I was dissatisfied with general theories of music therapy that make no distinction between clients, as if the characteristics of the disease are unimportant and as if using music therapy means applying the same therapeutic techniques to different groups of clients. I therefore used categories of diseases and developed some general treatment guidelines for specific diseases, thus "separating data from people." Now I understand better a comment one music therapist made during the round-table on indications at the World Congress in Hamburg in 1996. She criticized my "medical" point of view, somehow pointing out my shortcomings concerning unique subjectivity. A music therapist never treats the depression but an individual person who feels depressed. Rogers (1993) tells us we should acknowledge that ". . . clients or research subjects will not fit into a neatly labeled subject group." Therefore, as Payne (1993) puts it, we should not do research *on* clients but *with* and *for* clients.

Should we go back to the general theory of music therapy and neglect categories of diseases? I think not. When we focus on categories of diseases, however, we should never forget that general laws, rules, and guidelines are abstractions made from the study of individual people who experience their life within an individual context and can tell us their "knowledge" about life. We should not exclude standardized assessments, because they, too, can tell us something and make comparisons possible. We should not forget, either, that ". . . not all individuals behave idiosyncratically" (Aldridge, 1996a), yet we should take care that we are open to what cannot be standardized.

Aldridge calls it a myth that to know anything we must be scientists. My piano teacher, when referring to people able to talk about piano playing but unable to play, often asked, "They know a lot, but what do they really know?" During my therapeutic studies, I had very bad feelings about students who intellectually knew a lot about theories about human beings but were unable to grasp subjective knowledge of individual human beings. In music therapy, we should take care that theories do not replace human beings. Qualitative single-case studies can protect us from doing this. I feel an affinity with Aldridge's belief that ". . . knowledge about being human is not restricted to instrumentation through machines. . . . Knowledge is something that can be sung or played or danced or acted . . ." (Aldridge, 1996b). I believe this is the core "truth" of all arts therapies. We should take care that we do not using the psychiatrist's and psychotherapist's verbal language and frame of reference. Expression and communication through the arts, by painting, making music, dancing and moving, and acting is a different way of knowing. There should be a bridge to the language of psychotherapy and psychiatry, but we should not reduce the experiences of arts therapies by reframing them in nonaesthetic terminology. Arts therapists work in the field of psychotherapy and psychiatry, but they should not act and communicate as verbal psychotherapists and psychiatrists.

Ruud (1996c) shows us a triangle of description, effect, and interpretation in which he thinks different paradigms of research can be located. He then makes a distinction between:

- Pragmatic descriptive research: obtaining "correct" behavioral data and intersubjectively shared statements
- Pragmatic effect research: searching for "truth" by behavioral outcomes
- Positivistic descriptive research: claiming correspondence with reality by making detailed descriptions of musical parameters
- Revealing the nature of the phenomenon: investigating the experiences of the client, not fully recognizing the meaning is a construct
- Hermeneutics: constructing, by means of interpretation, a deeper underlying theme or meaning
- Narrative and rhetorical knowledge: deconstructing "the meaning behind"; not constructing a deeper meaning of the music but describing the music in the

context of the musical code developed throughout the previous sessions

This is a valuable contribution to our understanding of research paradigms. In his triangle, the most important criterion is the use of "truth": truth as pragmatic consequence, as correspondence with reality, and as constructed (metaphoric) representation. Some points are less clear and may lead to future discussions. For instance, Ruud contends that phenomenology belongs to the third category, which is surely an astonishing conclusion because phenomenologists claim that they are representatives of the qualitative research paradigm. Ruud tells us that on the contrary, they are searching for "the essence," that they come close to holding a positivistic standard of truth and are using the paradigm of naive realism. He may be right about some phenomenologists' statements, but Forinash and Gonzales's studies (see Chapter 4) do not, in my opinion, exclude the individual subjective experience or claim universal truth. I think the connection between "essence" and "experience"—the fact that quantitative research excludes experience—is more important in their perspective than the statement that it is "the" essence. As I said in Chapter 4, the way reality is perceived, how it becomes a phenomenon in the person, is paramount in phenomenology, not "the" reality; this distinction should be a topic of discussion among phenomenologists in the future. I am not sure whether all prominent qualitative research methods are adequately described by Ruud's triangle. Category 4, for instance, can be used for grounded theory but cannot include Lincoln and Guba's naturalistic inquiry because the latter explicitly uses constructed realities. Perhaps Ruud should explain how the research methods described here fit into his triangle.

TOPICS IN THE DISCUSSION OF QUALITATIVE RESEARCH

Several researchers who took part in the discussion in Düsseldorf met in Berlin just before the 1996 World Congress in Hamburg. They continued their discussion and brought their ideas to the round-table on qualitative research at the World Congress. Some of the themes were:

- How to create a research culture
- How to establish trust within a community of researchers
- How to deal with subjectivity: how "personal" can research be, and what can be published?
- How to find the right balance between outcome and process research

This section lists some topics that I believe have been and still are main focus points in the discussion about quantitative and qualitative research in music therapy. They were presented after the round-table meeting.

Quantitative versus Qualitative:
- Should the qualitative paradigm be the only paradigm for doing research in music therapy because it can describe the essence of music therapy? What is this essence?
- What can be accomplished by quantitative research?
- Do qualitative research criteria differ fundamentally from quantitative criteria or is it possible to connect them to such criteria as "reliability" and "validity"?

Objectivity–Subjectivity:
- How can the researcher's "subjectivity" be used as a research tool and how can it be controlled? Should it be controlled?
- How should the researcher's selection, conceptualization, and categorization of the data be controlled? Should there be a list of data that have been left out?
- How can a researcher really be open to the unexpected?
- Is it possible for a researcher to control his or her own inauthenticity?
- Should there be just one person who at the same time is both the music therapist and the researcher? Is doing research the same as providing treatment?
- Should it be possible for an independent researcher or research team to track the chain of evidence during or after research?
- Should a research team strive for intersubjectivity—some sort of shared interpretation—or should there be multiple perspectives, a cumulation of distinct aspects?

- Do the client's subjective experiences correspond with changes in pathology?
- How does the researcher regulate his or her attempt to interpret the client's inner thoughts and feelings in constructs?
- Is it possible to use the researcher's experience of the client's experience as a multiple perspective?
- Can there be full equality between researcher and client?

Theory:
- What is the role of already-existing theories?
- How can qualitative researchers be open without biasing their data by theoretical preconceptions?
- How can the researcher's personal values be made explicit?
- Should a qualitative researcher, when interpreting, be eclectic?
- Should the research employ preexisting categories or should categories emerge from the data?
- If there is no "truth," no "human laws," how can a music therapist develop a treatment method?
- Should a qualitative researcher—because he or she is researching experience—root his or her work in humanistic therapy?
- Is a qualitative researcher allowed to select those incidents that support his or her interpretation?

Research Rules and Techniques:
- Are there some basic rules for doing qualitative research or is the methodology of qualitative research completely open?
- Are master clinicians researchers?
- What are appropriate techniques for qualitative research?
- Are there techniques that can be used in several types of research?
- Can the traditional case study be a qualitative research method?
- Can supervision be part of qualitative research?
- Is doing qualitative research like improvising?
- Should there be research while therapy is in progress?

Process:
- Should qualitative research focus on one complete improvisation, on segments of several improvisations, or on all improvisations?
- How does the researcher solve the problem of time-consuming procedures?

Naturalism and Generalization:
- Can the findings of one particular case be generalized?
- How does the researcher solve the problem that because the client knows he or she is being studied, the setting is not natural?

Cause and Effect:
- Should cause and effect be used in qualitative research because clients themselves think in terms of cause and effect?
- Are conditions like causes and functions like effects?

Society:
- Should there be quantitative effect research because society wants it?
- Should research have relevance for music therapy practice?
- Should we, as music therapy researchers, develop our own language?

EPILOGUE

I hope this book will enable students, music therapists, and researchers to conduct research in a way that does not interfere with treatment and that they will share with all of us their findings concerning what clients and music therapists experience when they share the music-therapy space. Doing qualitative research myself and studying the research methods my colleagues use was an intriguing, exciting expedition into the cosmos of insight, intuition, inspiration, consciousness, and self-insight. I thank my colleagues for this wealth of experience.

I will close with a personal story. As I mentioned before, I like going for a walk in the forests of my native country. It is beautiful, with hills, woods, little brooks, and black-beam houses that have been painted white. I feel at home there; it is a place I want to live and where I want to one day die. Years ago, I bought a book about this region. When it is cold in the winter, I take the book to bed and read it, daydreaming about spring, summer, and fall, the seasons when I will be drifting through the countryside. In the book, there is a picture of an old woman cooking the custards so typical of this part of the country. She is paying a great deal of attention to her hands as she kneads the dough for the custard cup. Perhaps she is unable to write down what she is doing, but this woman knows how to cook a custard: her face, her hands, her whole body know. It is a knowledge from inside, a knowledge of doing; any words she used would give us only an outsider's knowledge.

There is the same difference between being in the music and writing about the music, between experiencing another person and writing about your communication with that person. We as researchers will never be able to bring precisely into words what is felt in the music, what can happen within and between people. We never should forget that making theories about phenomena is not the same as experiencing these phenomena.

REFERENCES

Aigen K (1993). The music therapist as qualitative researcher. *Music Therapy* 12(1):16–39.

Aigen K (1995a). Here we are in music: one year with an adolescent, creative music therapy group. Nordoff-Robbins Music Therapy Monograph Series. New York University.

Aigen K (1995b). Interpretational research. In Wheeler BL (ed): *Music therapy research: quantitative and qualitative perspectives*. Phoenixville, PA: Barcelona Publishers.

Aigen K (1995c). Principles of qualitative research. In Wheeler BL (ed): *Music therapy research: quantitative and qualitative perspectives*. Phoenixville, PA: Barcelona Publishers.

Aigen K (1996a). The role of values in qualitative music therapy research. In Langenberg M, Aigen K, Frommer J (eds): *Qualitative music therapy research: beginning dialogues*. Gilsum, NH: Barcelona Publishers.

Aigen K (1996b). The researcher's cultural identity. In Langenberg M, Aigen K, and Frommer J (eds): *Qualitative music therapy research: beginning dialogues*. Gilsum, NH: Barcelona Publishers.

Aldridge D (1993). Music therapy research II: research methods suitable for music therapy. *The Arts in Psychotherapy* 20:117–131.

Aldridge D (1994). Single-case research designs for the creative arts therapist. *The Arts in Psychotherapy* 21:333–342.

Aldridge D (1996a). Music therapy research and practice in medicine: from out of the silence. London: Jessica Kingsley Publishers.

Aldridge D (1996b). Towards the development of a European research culture. In Pedersen IN, Bonde LO (eds): *Music therapy within multidisciplinary teams: proceedings of the third European Music Therapy Conference, Ålborg, June 1995*. Ålborg, Denmark: Ålborg Universitetsforlag.

Amir D (1990). A song is born: discovering meaning in improvised songs through phenomenological analysis of two music therapy sessions with a traumatic spinal-cord injured young adult. *Music Therapy* 9:62–81.

Amir D (1992). Awakening and expanding the self: meaningful moments in the music therapy process as experienced and described by music therapists and music therapy clients. Unpublished doctoral dissertation. New York University.

Amir D (1993). Moments of insight in the music therapy experience. *Music Therapy* 12(1):85–100.

Amir D (1996a). Experiencing music therapy: meaningful moments in the music therapy process. In Langenberg M, Aigen K, Frommer J (eds): *Qualitative music therapy research: beginning dialogues.* Gilsum, NH: Barcelona Publishers.

Amir D. (1996b). Issues in qualitative research: a personal journey. In Langenberg M, Aigen K, Frommer J (eds): *Qualitative music therapy research: beginning dialogues.* Gilsum, NH: Barcelona Publishers.

Bogdan R, Biklen SK (1982). Qualitative research for education: an introduction to theory and method. Boston: Allyn & Bacon.

Bruscia KE (1987). *Improvisational models of music therapy.* Springfield, IL: Charles C Thomas.

Bruscia KE (1995a). Differences between quantitative and qualitative research paradigms: implications for music therapy. In Wheeler B (ed): *Music therapy research: quantitative and qualitative perspectives.* Phoenixville, PA: Barcelona Publishers.

Bruscia KE (1995b). Modes of consciousness in guided imagery and music (GIM): a therapist's experience of the guiding process. In Kenny CB (ed): *Listening, playing, creating: essays on the power of sound.* Albany: State University of New York Press.

Bruscia KE (1995c). The process of doing qualitative research. Part I: Introduction. In Wheeler B (ed): *Music therapy research: quantitative and qualitative perspectives.* Phoenixville, PA: Barcelona Publishers.

Bruscia KE (1995d). The process of doing qualitative research. Part II: Procedural steps. In Wheeler B (ed): *Music therapy research: quantitative and qualitative perspectives.* Phoenixville, PA: Barcelona Publishers.

Bruscia KE (1995e). The process of doing qualitative research. Part III: The human side. In Wheeler B (ed): *Music therapy research: quantitative and qualitative perspectives.* Phoenixville, PA: Barcelona Publishers.

Bruscia KE (1995f). Topics, phenomena, and purposes in qualitative research. In Wheeler B (ed): *Music therapy research: quantitative and qualitative perspectives.* Phoenixville, PA: Barcelona Publishers.

Bruscia KE (1996a). Authenticity issues in qualitative research process. In Langenberg M, Aigen K, Frommer J (eds): *Qualitative music therapy research: beginning dialogues.* Gilsum, NH: Barcelona Publishers.

Bruscia KE (1996b). Daedalus and the labyrinth: a mythical research fantasy. In Langenberg M, Aigen K, Frommer J (eds): *Qualitative music therapy research: beginning dialogues.* Gilsum, NH: Barcelona Publishers.

Campbell DT, Stanley JC (1966). Experimental and quasi-experimental designs for research. Chicago: Rand McNally.

Colaizzi PF (1978). Psychological research as the phenomenologist views it. In Valle RS, King M (eds): *Existential phenomenological alternatives for psychology.* New York: Oxford University Press.

Cook TD, Campbell DT (1979). Quasi-experimentation: design and analysis issues for field settings. Boston: Houghton Mifflin.

Czogalik D (1996). Das Heidelberger IMDoS Projekt: Zum Verbund von Forschung, Praxis und Ausbildung im Berufsfeld Musiktherapie. In Bolay HV (Hrsg): *Grundlagen zur Musiktherapieforschung.* Stuttgart: Gustav Fischer Verlag.

Czogalik D, Bozo M, Birringer S, Schauermann H, Jungaberle HE, Hänsel MF (1995). Zum Verlauf bedeutsamer Episoden in einer Musiktherapie: Ein Beispiel aus dem Integrativen Musiktherapie-Dokumentationssystem IMDoS. *Musiktherapeutische Umschau* 16(4):270–288.

Ely M, Anzul M, Friedman T, Garner D, McGormack Steinmetz A (1995). *Doing qualitative research: circles within circles.* London: The Falmer Press.

Ferrara L (1984). Phenomenology as a tool for musical analysis. *The Musical Quarterly* 70(3):355–373.

Forinash M (1990). A phenomenology of music therapy with the terminally ill. *Dissertation Abstracts International* 51(9):2915A.

Forinash M (1992). A phenomenological analysis of Nordoff-Robbins approach to music therapy: the lived experience of clinical improvisation. *Music Therapy* 11:120–141.

Forinash M (1993). An exploration into qualitative research in music therapy. *The Arts in Psychotherapy* 20:69–73.

Forinash M (1995). Phenomenological research. In Wheeler BL (ed): *Music therapy research: quantitative and qualitative perspectives.* Phoenixville, PA: Barcelona Publishers.

Forinash M, Gonzalez D (1989). A phenomenological perspective of music therapy. *Music Therapy* 8(1):35–46.

Frohne-Hagemann I (1995). Integrative Musiktherapie bei Menschen mit depressiven Zuständen. *Musiktherapeutische Umschau* 16(1):16–31.

Frommer J (1997). Gütekriterien qualitativer Psychotherapieforschung. In Bolay HV (Hsrg): *Wissenschaftliche Annäherungen an ein weites Feld. Heidelberger Schriften zur Musiktherapie, Band 11.* Stuttgart: Gustave Fischer Verlag.

Garner D (1986). An ethnographic study of four 5-year-old children's play styles. Doctoral dissertation. New York University.

Giorgi A. (1984). A phenomenological psychological analysis of the artistic process. In Gilbert J (ed): *Qualitative evaluation in the arts, II.* New York: New York University School of Education, Health, Nursing and Arts Professions.

Giorgi A (1985). Sketch of a psychological phenomenological method. In: *Phenomenology and psychological research.* Pittsburgh: Duquesne University Press.

Glaser BG, Strauss AL (1967). *The discovery of grounded theory.* Chicago: Aldine.

Gonzalez D (1992). Mythopoeic music therapy: a phenomenological investigation into its application with adults. *Dissertation Abstracts International* 53(8):4371B.

Gonzalez D (1996). Activating myths: Mythopoeic music therapy in the training of music therapists. Paper presented at the 8th World Congress of Music Therapy, Hamburg.

Greenberg LS (1986). Research strategies. In Greenberg LS, Pinsof WM (eds): *The psychotherapeutic process: a research handbook.* New York: Guilford Press.

Guba EG, Lincoln YS (1982). Epistemological and methodological bases of naturalistic inquiries. *Educational Communication and Technology Journal* 30:233–252.

Guba EG, Lincoln YS (1989). *Fourth generation evaluation.* Newbury Park, CA: Sage Publications.

Hanser SB (1987). *Music therapist's handbook.* St. Louis: Warren H. Green.

Hanser SB (1995). Applied behavior analysis. In Wheeler BL (ed): *Music therapy research: quantitative and qualitative perspectives.* Phoenixville, PA: Barcelona Publishers.

Hanser SB, Wheeler BL (1995). Experimental research. In Wheeler BL (ed): *Music therapy research: quantitative and qualitative perspectives.* Phoenixville, PA: Barcelona Publishers.

Hesser B (1982). Research position paper. In Hesser B (ed): *Unpublished proceedings from the International Symposium on Music in the Life of Man.* New York: New York University.

Hilliard RB (1993). Single-case methodology in psychotherapy process and outcome research. *Journal of Consulting and Clinical Psychology* 61(3):373–380.

Horkheimer M, Adorno TW (1981). *Dialektik der Aufklärung.* Frankfurt: Fischer Taschenbuch Verlag.

Hutjes JM, van Buuren JA (1992). *De gevalsstudie.* Meppel: Boom.

Janke W, Debus G (1971). *Die Eigenschafts-Wörterliste.* Göttingen: Hogrefe.

Kazdin AE (1986a). Research designs and methodology. In Garfield SL, Bergin AE (eds): *Handbook of psychotherapy and behavior change.* New York: Guilford Press.

Kazdin AE (1986b). The evaluation of psychotherapy: research and methodology. In Garfield SL, Bergin AE (eds): *Handbook of psychotherapy and behavior change.* New York: John Wiley & Sons.

Kenny CB (1989). *The field of play: a guide for the theory and practice of music therapy.* California: Atascadero.

Kenny CB (1996a). The story of the field of play. In Langenberg M, Aigen K, Frommer J (eds): *Qualitative music therapy research. Beginning dialogues.* Gilsum, NH: Barcelona Publishers.

Kenny CB (1996b). Remembering what's between the lines. In Langenberg M, Aigen K, Frommer J (eds): *Qualitative music therapy research: beginning dialogues.* Gilsum, NH: Barcelona Publishers.

Kiesler DJ (1983). The paradigm shift in psychotherapy process research. Summary discussant paper. Presented at the National Institute of Mental Health Workshop on Psychotherapy Process Research, Bethesda, MD.

Kühn TS (1975). *The structure of scientific revolutions.* Chicago: University of Chicago Press.

Küng M (1995). Introduction to morphological research. Unpublished paper.

Langenbach M, Stratkötter A (1996). Qualitative methods in music therapy research: epistemological considerations. In Langenberg M, Aigen K, Frommer J (eds): *Qualitative music therapy research: beginning dialogues.* Gilsum, NH: Barcelona Publishers.

Langenberg M, Frommer J, Langenbach M (1996). Fusion and separation: experiencing opposites in music, music therapy and music therapy research. In Langenberg M, Aigen K, Frommer J (eds): *Qualitative music therapy research: beginning dialogues.* Gilsum, NH: Barcelona Publishers.

Langenberg M, Frommer J, Tress W (1992). Qualitative Methodik zur Beschreibung und Interpretation musiktherapeutischer Behandlungswerke. *Musiktherapeutische Umschau* 13:258–278.

Langenberg M, Frommer J, Tress W (1993). A qualitative research approach to analytical music therapy. *Music Therapy* 12(1):59–84.

Lathom-Radocy WB, Radocy RE (1995). Descriptive quantitative research. In Wheeler BL (ed): *Music therapy research: quantitative and qualitative perspectives.* Phoenixville, PA Barcelona Publishers.

Lee CA (1989). Structural analysis of therapeutic improvisatory music. *Psychology of Music* 16:26–41.

Lee CA (1990). Structural analysis of post-tonal therapeutic improvisatory music. *Journal of British Music Therapy* 4:6–20.

Lee CA (1992). The analysis of therapeutic improvisatory music with people living with the HIV virus and AIDS. Unpublished doctoral thesis. London: City University.

Lee C (1995). The analysis of therapeutic improvisatory music. In Gilroy A, Lee C (eds): *Art and music: therapy and research*. London: Routledge.

Lee CA (1996). A method of analyzing improvisations in music therapy. Paper presented at the 8th World Congress of Music Therapy, Hamburg.

Lincoln YS, Guba EG (1985). Doing what comes naturally. In: *Naturalistic inquiry*. Newbury Park, CA: Sage Publications.

Luborsky L, Kächele H (1988). *Der zentrale Beziehungskonflikt*. Ulm, Germany: PSZ-Verlag.

Maso I (1989). *Kwalitatief onderzoek*. Meppel: Boom.

Mayring P (1990). *Qualitative Inhaltsanalyse: Grundlagen und Techniken*. Weinheim: Deutscher Studien Verlag.

Miles MB, Huberman AM (1984). *Qualitative data analysis: a sourcebook of new methods*. Newbury Park, CA: Sage Publications.

Nordoff P, Robbins C (1977). *Creative music therapy*. New York: John Day & Co.

Osborne JW (1989). A phenomenological investigation of the musical representation of extra-musical ideas. *Journal of Phenomenological Psychology* 20(2):151–175.

Pavlicevic M (1989). Dynamic interplay in clinical improvisation. *Journal of British Music Therapy* 4:5–9.

Payne H (1993). From practitioner to researcher: research as a learning process. In: *Handbook of inquiry in the arts therapies: one river, many currents*. London: Jessica Kingsley Publishers.

Racker H (1968). *Transference and countertransference*. New York: International University Press.

Remmert C (1992). Wirkungsforschung in der Musiktherapie: Ein Beispiel Teil I. *Musik-, Tanz-, und Kunsttherapie* 3:125–128.

Rogers P (1993). Research in music therapy with sexually abused clients. In Payne H (ed): *Handbook of inquiry in the arts therapies: one river, many currents.* London: Jessica Kingsley Publishers.

Rowan J, Reason P (1991). On making sense. In Reason P, Rowan J (eds): *Human inquiry. A sourcebook of new paradigm research.* Chichester, England: John Wiley & Sons.

Ruud E (1996a). Music therapy as a science: a narrative perspective. In Summer L (ed): *Music therapy international report.* Vol. 10. Ossining, NY: American Association for Music Therapy.

Ruud E (1996b). Interpretation and epistemology in music therapy *or* how to deal with competing claims of knowledge. In Langenberg M, Aigen K, Frommer J (eds): *Qualitative music therapy research: beginning dialogues.* Gilsum, NH: Barcelona Publishers.

Ruud E (1996c): Music therapy: the science of interpretation. In Pedersen IN, Bonde LO (eds): *Music therapy within multidisciplinary teams: proceedings of the third European Music Therapy Conference, Ålborg, June 1995.* Ålborg, Denmark: Ålborg Universitetsforlag.

Salber W (1960). Qualitative Methoden der Persönlichkeitsforschung. In: *Handbuch der Psychologie.* Bd. 4. Göttingen: Hogrefe.

Salber W (1965). *Morphologie des seelischen Geschehens.* Ratingen.

Schirmer H, Hupfeld A (1988). "Zwischen Himmel und Erde." Der Versuch, die Musik von psychotischen und neurotischen Patientengruppen in ihrem Wesen zu verstehen. *Musiktherapeutische Umschau* 9:214–225.

Smaling A (1995). Open-mindedness, open-heartedness and dialogical openness: the dialectics of openings and closures. In Maso I, Atkinson PA, Delamont S, Verhoeven JC (eds): *Openness in research.* Assen: Van Gorcum.

Smeijsters H (1993). Music therapy and psychotherapy. *The Arts in Psychotherapy.* 20:223–229.

Smeijsters H (1996a). Analogy as a core category of music therapy. Paper presented at the 8th World Congress of Music Therapy, Hamburg.

Smeijsters H (1996b). Entweder—oder? Überlegungen zur quantitativen und qualitativen Forschung in der Musiktherapie. *Musiktherapeutische Umschau* 17(1):23–38.

Smeijsters H (1996c). Qualitative research in music therapy: new contents, new concepts, or both? A dialogue. In Pedersen IN, Bonde LO (eds): *Music therapy within multi-disciplinary teams*. Ålborg, Denmark: Ålborg Unifersitetsforlag.

Smeijsters H (1996d). Qualitative research in music therapy: new contents, new concepts, or both? In Langenberg M, Aigen K, Frommer J (eds): *Qualitative music therapy research: beginning dialogues*. Gilsum, NH: Barcelona Publishers.

Smeijsters H (1996e). Qualitative single-case research in practice: a necessary, reliable, and valid alternative for music therapy research. In Langenberg M, Aigen K, Frommer J (eds): *Qualitative music therapy research: beginning dialogues*. Gilsum, NH: Barcelona Publishers.

Smeijsters H (in press). Analogy as a core category of music therapy. In: *Proceedings of the World Congress of Music Therapy*. Hamburg.

Smeijsters H (in preparation). Powerless metaphors: about symbol, metaphor and analogy in music therapy.

Smeijsters H, Rogers P (1993). European music therapy research register. Utrecht: Werkgroep Onderzoek Muziektherapie NVKT.

Smeijsters H, Rogers P, Kortegaard H-M, Lehtonen K, Scanlon P (eds). European music therapy research register. Volume II. Castricum: Stichting Muziektherapie.

Smeijsters H, Storm H (1997). Becoming friends with your mother: techniques of qualitative research illustrated with examples from the short-term treatment of a girl who wetted herself. *Music Therapy*.

Smeijsters H, van den Berk P (1995). Music therapy with a client suffering from musicogenic epilepsy: a naturalistic qualitative single-case research. *The Arts in Psychotherapy* 22(3):249–263.

Smeijsters H, van den Hurk J (1993). Research in practice in the music therapeutic treatment of a client with symptoms of anorexia nervosa. In Heal M, Wigram T (eds): *Music therapy in health and education*. London: Jessica Kingsley Publishers.

Smeijsters H, van den Hurk J (1994). Praxisorientierte Forschung in der Musiktherapie. *Musiktherapeutische Umschau* 15(1):25–42.

Smeijsters H, van den Hurk J (in press). Music therapy helping to work through grief and finding a personal identity: qualitative single-case research.

Standley JM, Prickett CA (eds) (1994). *Research in music therapy: a tradition of excellence. Outstanding reprints from the Journal of Music Therapy 1964–1993.* Silver Spring, National Association for Music Therapy.

Strauss AL (1991). *Qualitative analysis for social scientists.* Cambridge: Cambridge University Press.

Strauss A, Corbin J (1990). *Basics of qualitative research: grounded theory procedures and techniques.* Newbury Park, CA: Sage Publications.

Strupp HH (1960). *Psychotherapists in actions: explorations of the therapists' contribution to the treatment process.* New York: Grune.

Strupp HH (1990). The case of Helen R. *Psychotherapy* 27:644–656.

Taylor SJ, Bogdan R (1984). *Introduction to qualitative research methods: the search for meanings.* New York: John Wiley & Sons.

Tesch R (1992). *Qualitative research: analysis types and software tools.* New York: The Falmer Press.

Timmermann TN, Scheytt-Hölzer N, Bauer S, Kächele H (1991). Musiktherapeutische Einzelfall-Prozessrschung-Entwicklung und Aufbau eines Forschungsfeldes. *Psychotherapie, Psychosomatik und Medizinische Psychologie* 41:385–391.

Tüpker R (1983). Morphologische Arbeitsmethoden in der Musiktherapie. *Musiktherapeutisch Umschau* 4:247–264.

Tüpker R (1988). Ich singe, was ich nicht sagen kann: Zu einer morphologischen Grundlegung der Musiktherapie. Regensburg: Gustav Bosse Verlag.

Tüpker R (1990a). Auf der Suche nach angemessenen Formen wissenschaftlichen Vorgehens in kunsttherapeutischer Forschung. In Petersen P (Hrsg): *Ansätze kunsttherapeutischer Forschung.* Berlin: Springer-Verlag.

Tüpker R (1990b). Wissenschaftlichkeit in kunsttherapeutischer Forschung. *Musiktherapeutische Umschau* 11:7–20.

van Colle S, Williams T (1995). Starting out in music therapy process research. In Gilroy A, Lee C (eds): *Art and music: therapy and research*. London: Routledge.

van den Hurk J, Smeijsters H (1991). Musical improvisation in the treatment of a man with obsessive compulsive personality disorder. In Bruscia KE (ed): *Case studies in music therapy*. Phoenixville, PA: Barcelona Publishers.

Vanger P, Oerter U, Otto H, Schmidt S, Czogalik D (1995). The musical expression of the separation conflict during music therapy: a single-case study of a Crohn's disease patient. *The Arts in Psychotherapy* 22(2):147–154.

Wheeler B (ed) (1995). *Music therapy research: quantitative and qualitative perspectives*. Phoenixville, PA: Barcelona Publishers.

Yin RK (1989). Case study research: design and methods. Newbury Park, CA: Sage Publications.

INDEX

Ability(ies), natural, 61
Abstraction(s), 6, 7, 11, 15, 64, 116, 199, 204
  of emotion(s), 204
Accommodation, 17, 125, 127, 201
Acquired immunodeficiency syndrome (AIDS), 123, 168, 171
Action(s), 66, 146, 151, 181, 183
  orientation, 146
  research, 151, 181, 183
  strategy(ies) of, 66
Acupuncturist(s), 93
Adaptation, 26
Adorno, Theodor, 96, 98, 128, 195
Aesthetic(s), 99, 101, 102, 110, 191, 197, 203
Agreement, 35, 74
  averaged intersubjective, 35
  and cross-analysis(es), 74
  model(s), 74
AIDS; *see* Acquired immunodeficiency syndrome
Aigen, Ken, 8, 26, 27, 30, 39, 43, 81, 114, 121, 128, 135, 136, 137, 141, 142, 144, 145, 146, 147, 148, 149, 150, 167, 189, 190, 192, 193, 194, 196, 197, 198, 201, 202, 203
Aimee-Sawyer, 55, 56
Aldridge, David, 9, 27, 33, 36, 98, 178, 192, 193, 196, 197, 200, 203, 204, 205
Alliance(s), 160
Alternative, 19, 28, 29, 32
  explanation(s), 28, 29
  possibility(ies), 32
  suggestion(s), 19
Ambiguity(ies), 95, 98
Amir, Dorit, 27, 30, 59, 69, 70, 71, 78, 105, 106, 114, 190, 193, 198, 203
Analogy(ies), 21, 80, 84, 89, 104, 109, 110, 112, 114, 121, 140, 162, 163, 165, 197
  between music and motif(s), 109
  between consciousness shifts and music, 121
  paradigmatic, 80
  specific, 162
Analysis(es), 18, 19, 20, 22, 23, 33, 38, 53, 57, 58, 59, 60, 64, 71, 72, 73, 74, 74, 81, 89, 105, 107, 113, 114, 116, 117, 119, 120, 136,